THE UNIVERSAL CHARACTER
OF CHRISTIANITY

The Universal
Character of Christianity

by

A. K. CLARKE

FABER AND FABER LIMITED

24 Russell Square

London

*First published in mcml
by Faber and Faber Limited
24 Russell Square London W.C.1
Printed in Great Britain by
Latimer Trend & Co Ltd Plymouth*

CONTENTS

PREFACE

The genesis of this short book was a number of talks given to elder girls at the Cheltenham Ladies' College in 1937. In preparing the material for these talks I was especially helped by Dr. Hall's great work on Dogmatic Theology and by the writings of the late Baron von Hügel. I also found valuable help in *Elements of the Spiritual Life* (S.P.C.K., 1932) by the Rev. F. P. Harton, B.D. and in the writings of Father Thornton, C.R. The material has since been entirely recast and rewritten and in such a reshaping the influence of particular books naturally becomes less important, but I am still conscious of a special debt to these writers and I am glad to record it.

I am indeed grateful for the help that I have received from many quarters while writing this book. I owe especial thanks to the Rev. F. P. Harton, Master of the Mercers' Company (1949-50), and to Mrs. Harton, for their generous help and encouragement, without which the book would not have reached its present stage; and to Miss M. E. Popham, Principal of the Cheltenham Ladies' College, for her kindness in so arranging my work that I had time to complete it. I am very grateful to Mrs. J. H. Gettins ('Kathleen Campbell', the author of *Sarah, Duchess of Marlborough* and *Beau Brummell*) for the discerning criticism which she gave to the manuscript; and to Miss H. M. Simpson, O.B.E., Principal of Exhall Training College, Coventry, for her encouragement and valuable advice.

PREFACE

I should like to thank the Librarian of Dr. Williams's Library, and Miss V. M. Hounsfield, the Librarian of the Cheltenham Ladies' College, for their kindness in helping me to procure books and verify some references.

In attempting to write on this great subject I have not tried, or wished, to say anything new. Great truths are envisaged by each individual with a special form and colouring and it may sometimes happen that the way in which they are seen by one is useful to another. We

'help each other so,
Lending our minds out,'

and this is perhaps the chief justification for gathering stray leaves of thought into the form of a book. I had been inclined to dwell for many years on the universal quality of Christianity and especially on the two different ways in which it expresses itself in our experience. It penetrates every corner and cranny of human life and character, with the power to heal and to refashion whatever is there: it also corresponds perfectly, at a higher level, both with the natural religious consciousness of human beings, and with those capacities of reasoning and judgment by which man extends his experience beyond the impressions of his senses. In this second field I have ventured to believe that something still remains to be done by Christian thinkers. There seems a real need, not so much to express the Christian faith in modern philosophical terms, as to show where and how the most constructive thinking of the last few centuries is in a true harmony with Christian doctrine. Such work on the great scale could perhaps best be achieved by a group of thinkers working in close co-operation. It needs a profound and sympathetic knowledge of some very great minds, but also a fine intuition which can discern the positive element in much perverse or one-sided

8

thought, and distil its value. I need hardly say that this book does not attempt to make the smallest contribution to such a task, but the belief that it needs to be done by those qualified to undertake it, has been in the background of my mind.

The plan of the book was directed by these two lines of thought which I have mentioned. They are very closely related and I have made no attempt to keep them rigidly apart, but, broadly speaking, the first six chapters are concerned with the character of Christianity as a fulfilment of human nature and history, the last four with its work of penetration and remaking. The interdependence of the two seemed to be shown most clearly by considering them in this order. I had intended to add a chapter on some difficulties, other than the claim to universality, which have caused many thinking people to drift away from Christian doctrine. Dislike for the very conception of a body of doctrine is still widely felt and expressed, and this dislike is partly, perhaps, the result of misunderstanding. But although this subject is closely connected with the universal character of Christianity, it is *sui generis*. It seemed better to plan the book quite simply, as a comment upon some of the reasons for which the Christian religion can be called universal. Yet the reality and seriousness of these difficulties was often being brought home to me, in a number of ways, while the book was being written. Attempts, of the greatest value, have been made to meet them; but much of the finest theological work is discounted, or ignored, by those not already convinced of its truth, because it is based on assumptions, both historical and philosophical, which they do not share. The first difficulty here is perhaps the more easily met. Modern historical criticism has done a great work in examining the written sources and Christianity has nothing to fear from its conclusions. Though there is still a vast amount of work to be accomplished, it can fairly be said that the truth and authenticity of the documents stand more firmly based than ever. The metaphysical bases of Christianity are equally firm and sure, but they are greatly at variance with some present trends of thought. If for this reason alone, it is imperative to bring out clearly what they are and to show reasons for finding them valid. Thus what Dr. Farrer has called 'the spiritual importance of metaphysical thinking'[1] was being gradually borne in upon my mind while I was writing this book.

It seems, at first sight, impracticable to lay stress upon pure thinking in these very critical and anxious times. The greater part of our working energies must be thrown into practical action, if the needs of the moment are to be met. Yet periods of crisis, when the pressure of events is very great, can be favourable to thought. Comparisons are dangerous, but they can be valuable if not pressed too far. There seem some real resemblances between our own time and the stormy and catastrophic period of the fourth and fifth centuries in our era. A long-established and stable society was being threatened and perilous breaches driven deep into its structure. Parts of the civilized world which had been spared direct experience of war for many centuries were exposed to its horror and ruin; and a deliberate withdrawal from some long-held parts of the Empire had brought fresh anxieties and dangers. It might well hav/ seemed a time for the subordination of thought to action, and even for the restriction of action to the urgent demands of each day. In both directions, the response of the Church is surprising. It was a time of far-sighted daring in missionary enterprise, and a time when very great and enduring contributions were made to the expression of

[1] *The Glass of Vision.* Austin Farrer D.D. (Bampton Lectures for 1948), Lecture IV. p. 76.

PREFACE

Christian thought. We are the heirs of this achievement in both fields, and it is a cheering and encouraging example.

The presence of these different trains of thought has made the book something of a *satura* or hotch-potch; it is not wholly concerned with either history, or philosophy, or theology, but a little with all three. My only excuse is that much of our ordinary meditative thinking has this blended character. A certain common stock of such Christian thinking may be useful, even necessary, as the soil in which expert and original thought can flourish, and this book will have achieved its purpose if it can make a very small contribution to the common stock.

The chief beneficiary, however, from any book on a great theme is the author, who gains a wider view of the subject in the process of writing. A few leading points, perhaps, were seen clearly at the beginning. They are still there at the end, but something has been added, a fuller sense of horizon, and of the infinitude in which our minds can both work and rest.

A. K. CLARKE

Chapter One

INTRODUCTORY

The growth of a personal Christian faith comes easily and almost unconsciously to some people, but these perhaps are a minority. They may have been so fortunate as to grow up in a wise and stable religious environment: it has come naturally to them to take their faith, in the first instance, upon trust, and they have grown to realize it as their own by an almost imperceptible process. They could hardly have named the moment at which the one kind of belief passed into the other. But there are many for whom the passage from traditional to personal belief is less easy, and of these a great number become permanently entangled in misconceptions and never find their way to a full Christian faith. Many too, who have not been brought up as Christians but are attracted by Christianity, find themselves checked and alienated by apparent intellectual puzzles. The claim that Christianity is essentially a universal religion and that in Christ there is a final revelation of God is one of the greatest of difficulties, and this distrust of any claim to finality and primacy is felt most keenly by many who have a deep faith in God. They believe devoutly that He is and that He manifests Himself to all. They believe that the visible world around us, which feeds and clothes our bodies and by which our sense of beauty and need of spaciousness are at once nurtured and satisfied, can give us some indications of His Being and Nature. Many would go further, and maintain that

13

as man cannot be wholly satisfied through his senses, there is the probability of a Divine manifestation which will satisfy his other needs; that the mind and spirit of man, reaching out beyond its visible environment, finds a wider environment surrounding it which is a further revelation of God. They regard the great conceptions of value —Truth, Justice, Beauty, Goodness—as essentially such a manifestation. The origin of these ideas is admittedly complex and there can be no absolute partition of human experience: there is a deep interpenetration and interlocking of the senses and the intellect and it is impossible for us to isolate the spiritual from either. Yet this interpenetration is never quite identity, and it remains true that there are needs of man which outrange his sense-experience, but find repose and satisfaction in the great 'abstract' ideas. Whatever the immediate origin of these, they are felt to be of satisfying value; they are far more than mere abstract conceptions, and many would feel that the truest way to think of them is as Attributes of God, a part of the revelation of Himself.

This does not at first sight make the approach to Christianity easier. A Divine manifestation in what lies beyond the senses may be expected to have the same character in another form as is found in the world of nature—the presence, that is, of great, permanent, universal elements, such as air and light, together with a boundless flexibility and variety and power of adaptation. In revealing more of His inner Being than can be known through the senses, God will in the same way give Himself equally to all through certain great unchangeable characteristics. Yet there will also be infinite variations and adaptations to every kind of circumstance and need—to the spiritual climate, as it were, of every race and nation and every individual soul. God is always, and for all men, to be apprehended as Truth, Beauty, Goodness. Everything that the great value-judgments express at their highest and deepest, is the expression of what He is. The religions of mankind are fed and enlightened by these judgments as trees and plants are nourished by air and light. Like trees and plants they grow up and flower into a rich variety, and this variety is one great cause of beauty in both the natural and the spiritual world. A number of religions, showing common fundamental characteristics, but with many variations and with emphasis on different parts of truth, would thus seem to be the probable form of a Divine revelation, in the sphere of religious experience. It is not surprising that the claim of Christianity to be a universal religion and an ultimate revelation of God, often bewilders and estranges truly religious minds. The claim seems incompatible with their conception of God as Spirit, manifesting Himself equally, without distinction or reservation, to all mankind. Moreover, it is coupled with an emphasis on one Person, and on the necessity for certain beliefs about Him, which appears to limit free speculation for a Christian and so to fetter his individuality from the start. These are legitimate and natural perplexities, and they are centred on two questions which are different though closely related—on the possibility of a universal religion, and on the relation of Christianity, if truly universal, to the whole person and life. A satisfactory answer to the first question will go a long way towards answering the second, and if only for that reason it would deserve consideration.

For those who are still looking at Christianity from the outside there are many obvious difficulties. Why should there be one universal religion? It seems unnecessary to convert a good Jew, Hindu, Mohammedan, if they are already living out the highest implications of their own faith. To thrust the alien element of dogma into the wise and accomplished philosophy of Confucius, seems almost arrogance. Proselytizing appears an attempt, of the crudest kind, to standardize religious thought and experience. It need hardly be said that no completely satisfying answer to these questions can be found except in the light of Christian experience itself. This is not for lack of an answer which can satisfy the mind, but because the most complete intellectual satisfaction is necessarily inadequate. The whole person, not only the intelligence, is concerned in the adventure of faith, and the whole person must make it. But the approach to faith becomes easier through the removal of sincere difficulties, and these are often best met if they are looked at in a wide and uncontroversial setting. The whole religious principle in man, expressed everywhere in similar ideas and practices, and the highest faith and aspiration of non-Christian religions, can together provide such a background, against which the true character of Christianity stands out more clearly. The presence, over vast areas of space and time, of certain prevailing ideas and forms of experience is remarkable, even where the ideas are confined in their application to humanity, and to the visible and tangible; far more wonderful is the universality and similarity of that intuition which we call 'religious'—the sense of higher Power and the longing to establish relationship with It. This Power is not realized necessarily as Person, or even as One, or as Good, but only as Power, to be propitiated and feared. It is associated in the beginning with fear of natural forces, and sometimes identified with them: it is associated, and sometimes wholly or partially identified, with animals. Yet as man tamed or exterminated the animals, or survived them by his higher adaptability, and as he learnt to use and even master the natural forces around him, the sense of higher Power did not disappear. It grew, and was refined and deepened in the time-process, like other durable human qualities. Higher and more beautiful thought entered into it, among many peoples at different times: it was still a thought of some great Power to which man must relate himself rightly, but in varying degrees this Power was apprehended as one of goodness and beauty. The religious intuition, instead of being discarded in the evolutionary process as worthless, developed side by side with the rational powers, and established itself as one of the differentiating marks of humanity. It is at least a possibility worth consideration that this intuition which gropes for the unseen is the natural faculty by which man seeks God, and that it is as finely constructed and adapted for its special end as is the organ of sight for seeing. The faculty operates in three ways: in the sense of God's existence, in the desire to be in right contact with Him, and in the sense of awe: and like the other natural faculties, it has had a long upward history. From the birth of his consciousness man has been saying to God:

> *Holy, holy, holy! Though the darkness hide Thee,*
> *Though the eye of sinful man Thy glory may not see,*
> *Only Thou art Holy,*

though at first with only the dimmest perception of the real meaning of his words.

But the religious intuition, like all human gifts and powers, is capable of corruption; and the harm which any faculty, if wrongly used, can do, is in proportion to its importance. If man really possesses a faculty by means of which he can reach out to God, it will be enthroned at the very centre of his nature, and the result will be disastrous when so central a capacity is misused; even unavoidable ignorance here will have its consequences. If the Power

B 17

worshipped is wrongly conceived, worship will lead men to the very greatest crimes; this is so plainly written in history that it is not surprising if religion itself comes to be identified with its corruptions. Thus the deepest responsibility rests upon believers to seek for right ideas of God, and where this has been realized most fully, the curve of religious thought has moved swiftly upward; the religious consciousness, co-operating with reason, has gained a fresh expansion from a wider and nobler conception of the Object of its adoration. But it is not only the development of human reason which gradually purified the conception of the Power. The religious faculty, like the other primary human characteristics, is not working on a nothingness, but is directed towards a something beyond itself, which is its origin and the source of its progress. Religion is not like a game played for its own sake: in all its crudest formulae, incantations, sacrifices, ritual dances, man is reaching out beyond his natural surroundings and is seeking contact with the supernatural. The history of religious experience is the history of the answer given to his search. The evidence given by religious experience is later in time, and in its nature more indefinable and questionable than the evidence for the religious consciousness in man, but the two are in reality inseparable, and are interlocked in as close a unity as that of the visual sensation with the thing seen. It is not then surprising that history has to tell us not only of a search, but of a Finding, and that a weight of evidence supports the conclusion—already intrinsically likely—that God reveals Himself to man.

It is a privileged task to study this most beautiful of human attributes, the religious consciousness, at work; to watch it reaching out into the invisible and unknown, and receiving its answer in the form of a religious experience which becomes ever more deeply authenticated in the progress of time. It would be strange indeed if this answer were wholly local or particular, if it were given only to one people or one part of the globe. St. Paul, the greatest of all Christian missionaries, affirmed most confidently the universal character of Divine revelation. He took for granted, not merely the Divine self-disclosure in the visible universe, but that search which we have called tentatively the religious intuition, and the Finding which is religious experience: 'that they should seek God, if haply they might feel after Him and find Him'. The word ψηλα-φήσειαν means literally 'that they might grope for Him', as a man gropes for an unseen object in the dark; but he implies forcibly that it is no hopeless search. The invisible universe, though dark, is very near. 'καί γε οὐ μακρὰν ἀπὸ ἑνὸς ἑκάστου ἡμῶν ὑπάρχοντα.'[1] Finally he quotes the previous religious beliefs of his Greek hearers, as being valuable and true: 'ὡς καί τινες τῶν καθ' ὑμᾶς ποιητῶν εἰρήκασι, Τοῦ γὰρ καὶ γένος ἐσμέν.'[1]

St. Paul here provides the right starting-point. A preliminary study of ideas and beliefs entirely unconnected with historic Christianity, will place the Christian religion in its natural framework: it will help to show what religious ideas seem to be of universal occurrence and value. Some of the great non-Christian writings make us wonder whether there can or need be anything higher; such questioning is very valuable, if it leads us on to a deeper study of our inherited faith. There must be something, not only of transcendent beauty, but of unique character in the Christian revelation, if it is to exercise supreme authority over the highest thoughts of mankind.

[1] Acts xvii. 27, 28.

Chapter Two

THE DISPENSATION OF PAGANISM

The beautiful words of Philo, in commenting on the text 'Come up unto the Lord, thou and Aaron' are an admirable summary of the student's approach to religion. 'Go up, O soul, to the vision of Him who is: go up quietly, reasonably, willingly, fearlessly, lovingly.'—εὐαρμόστως, λογικῶς, ἑκουσίως, ἀφόβως, ἀγαπητικῶς.[1] The intellect must be used, and in an orderly and disciplined way; there must be an open-minded, fearless, unprejudiced outlook, and a real desire for the vision and understanding which is the object of search. Such a temper will naturally lead the Christian student to look for evidences of Divine revelation and of intercourse with God, wherever they are to be found, and to study them boldly and sympathetically.

To do this exhaustively would be a lifelong task, in which every part of the world would be brought under contribution. Two truths have emerged wherever such a study has been attempted: that religious belief exists independently in every part of the world, yet that this independence is woven into a close interdependence by the 'thread of continuity in human life and thought' and by the slow, yet wide and far-reaching diffusion of influences and ideas: this is especially true of the Mediterranean area where close contact has existed and seaborne communication has been open for a very long period of time. It is thus

---

[1] *De Migratione Abraham*, 31. The whole passage is very relevant and is quoted in Dr. Drummond's *Philo Judaeus*, vol. ii, chapter vi, pp. 250–1.

possible to trace the influence of Egypt and Chaldaea upon Greece and Palestine: to see the results of contact between Greece and Persia, and even between Greece and India, and the influence (at a later period) of Buddhism in the Graeco-Roman world. The purpose of this chapter is not to trace such influences, but to exhibit and illustrate the conceptions of the Divine Being and character, found outside the influence of developed Judaism and long before the Christian era. The richest field for such illustration is the ancient literature of India, Persia, and Greece, and some of these great writings should be within the normal range of Christian studies. They provide, not so much that general evidence for religious experience which the whole field of primitive religions can also give, but our best material for studying the development of thought about God Himself, His Being and Nature, and His relationship with man. In this lies their greatest value, and the quotations which follow are chosen to illustrate this development, and particularly at its highest and deepest range. They could be modified and qualified by many other passages from the same writings, showing a lower and weaker level of religious thought and sensibility: but when every qualification has been made, they leave us with an enlarged horizon, and with a most beautiful picture of God and man in intercourse from the very dawn of history. 'Olympus is but the outside of the earth everywhere.' The angels of God are forever ascending and descending, and there is a Bethel wherever there is an earth and sky.

The thousand hymns of the Rig-Veda, which are the earliest specimen of Indian religious thought, date from approximately 1400–1000 B.C., but they are of much older origin. Their personified nature-gods were worshipped, it seems certain, long before the Aryan migrations, and are

Indo-European, not merely Indian. Most of the Vedic hymns are very simple expressions of worship addressed to these personified natural forces; they are full of metaphor and picture, and teach us how long a history lies behind the Greek gods of Homer with their clearly defined epithets and characteristics. The anthropomorphism of the Rig-Veda is less sharply outlined than in Homer, but it is the same conception at an earlier stage, and however crude, is full of fresh and living beauty. But here and there, in some of the hymns, there is a suggestion—it can hardly be called more—of monotheistic thought. It appears sporadically, as a transient ascription of supreme power to one or other of the great nature gods, or as a sense of unity and dependence in all creation. Even if the hymns in which these passages occur are among the later of the collection, they are still early evidence, as far as they go, for the sense of an ever-existing Supreme Being underlying the multiform personification which is more constant and conspicuous. The worship of natural powers sprang readily from everyday observation and experience; the actual experience of pleasure, pain or danger from the surrounding forces of nature, led easily to feelings of gratitude or dread. But the belief in God as one and supreme was not based on data given by the senses: here if anywhere, rather than in the worship of the mythological divinities, we have the essence of the religious consciousness itself, and it is not surprising that it is so faintly and varyingly manifested.

The hymn to the 'Golden Germ', often quoted in this connection, is a late but genuine Vedic hymn:

'In the beginning there arose the Golden Child: as soon as born, he alone was the Lord of all that is. He stablished the earth and this heaven. Who is the God to whom we shall offer sacrifice? . . . He to whom heaven and earth, standing firm by His will, look up, trembling in their mind; He over whom the risen sun shines forth: Who is the God to whom we shall offer sacrifice? . . . May He not hurt us, He who is the begetter of the earth, or He, the righteous, who begat the heavens; He who also begat the light and mighty waters: Who is the God to whom we shall offer sacrifice?'[1]

Many of the hymns to Varuna—originally the encompassing sky—are earlier, but show clearly not only a potential monotheism, but the desire for communion and the sense of sin.

'Intelligent indeed are the generations by the might of Him who has propped asunder even the two wide worlds. He has pushed away the high lofty firmament, and the day-star as well; and He spread out the earth.

'And I converse thus with myself: "When, pray, shall I be in communion with Varuna? What oblation of mine would he, free from wrath, enjoy? When shall I, of good cheer, perceive His mercy?

'I ask about that sin, Varuna, with a desire to find out; I approach the wise in order to ask; the sages say one and the same thing to me: "This Varuna is wroth with thee."

'What has been that chief sin, O Varuna, that thou desirest to slay thy praiser, a friend? Proclaim that to me, thou that are hard to deceive, self-dependent one: thee would I, free from sin, eagerly appease with adoration.

'Set us free from the misdeeds of our fathers, from those that we have committed by ourselves.'[2]

There is the beginning of a philosophy of creation in the later part of the Rig-Veda, and a sense of the mystery

[1] *Sacred Books of the East*, vol. xxxii (Oxford, 1891), Vedic Hymns, Part I (trans. Max Müller) pp. 1-2, Mandala X, Hymn 121.
[2] *A Vedic Reader*, A. A. Macdonnell (Oxford, 1917), pp. 135-8.

of being which reaches out beyond the gods as visibly conceived.

'There was not the non-existent nor the existent then; there was not the air nor the heaven which is beyond. What did it contain? Where? In whose protection? Was there water, unfathomable, profound?

'There was not death nor immortality then. There was not the beacon of night, nor of day. That one breathed, windless, by its own power. Other than that there was not anything beyond.

'Whence this creation has arisen; whether he founded it or did not: he who in the highest heaven is its surveyor, he only knows, or else he knows not.'[1]

These tentative intimations of being and greatness and of a mysterious underlying unity, found a fuller expression in the Upanishads. Later than the Rig-Veda, they are still an ancient monument of pre-Christian religious thought, mainly dating from about the sixth century before Christ. The earlier Upanishads are not far removed in outlook from the later hymns of the Rig-Veda: the later are an elaborate expression of Brahmanic Pantheism, by which the Supreme Atman or World-Soul is identified with the principle of all things, Brahma: and Brahma is to be sought within.

'Verily, this whole world is Brahma. Tranquil, let one worship. . . . He who consists of mind, whose body is life, whose form is light, whose conception is truth, whose soul is space, containing all works, containing all desires, containing all odours, containing all tastes, encompassing this whole world, the unspeaking, the unconcerned—this Soul of mine within the heart is smaller than a grain of rice, or

[1] id. pp. 207–8, 211. A fine free translation of this passage will be found in *Hinduism*, by Sir Monier Monier-Williams (S.P.C.K., 1906), chapter ii, p. 26.

a barley-corn, or a mustard-seed, or a grain of millet, or the kernel of a grain of millet: this Soul of mine within the heart is greater than the earth, greater than the atmosphere, greater than the sky, greater than these worlds.

'Containing all works, containing all desires, containing all odours, containing all tastes, encompassing the whole world, the unspeaking, the unconcerned—this is the Soul of mine within the heart, this is Brahma. Into him I shall enter on departing hence.'[1]

It is easy to see the flaws in the Upanishads and to feel that their beauty is often vitiated by a crude and repellent Pantheism, but often, too, they rise far above their own ordinary level, in passages of great religious depth and insight. The grand simplicity and dignity of these passages give, taken alone, a very incomplete and even misleading idea of the Upanishads as a whole; but they provide un-questionable evidence for great conceptions of the Nature and Being of God, fully formed and expressed many centuries before the Christian era, and far removed from Palestine.

'Him who is the One Existent, sages name variously,' says one of the Vedic hymns; and many passages in the Upanishads, perhaps especially the earlier, emphasize the encompassing power and identity of God, and His entire supremacy over the Universe.

'Verily, O Gargi, at the command of that Imperishable the sun and moon stand apart. Verily, O Gargi, at the command of that Imperishable the earth and the sky stand apart. Verily, O Gargi, at the command of that Imperishable the moments, the hours, the days, the nights, the fortnights, the months, the seasons, and the years, stand

---

[1] *The Thirteen Principal Upanishads*, R. E. Hume (Oxford, 1931), pp. 209–10. Chāndogya Upanishad, 3, 14, 1, 2–4 (with some omissions).

apart. Verily, O Gargi, at the command of that Imperishable one river flows from the snowy mountains to the east, others to the west, in whatever direction each flows . . .

'Verily, O Gargi, that Imperishable is the Unseen Seer, the Unheard Hearer, the Unthought Thinker, the Ununderstood Understander. Other than It there is naught that sees. Other than It there is naught that hears. Other than It there is naught that thinks. Other than It there is naught that understands. Across this Imperishable, O Gargi, is space woven, warp and woof.'[1]

He is beyond the grasp of the senses, or the intellect:

> Not by speech, not by mind,
> Not by sight can He be apprehended.
> How can He be comprehended
> Otherwise than by saying 'He is'?[2]

Though the main emphasis is laid throughout on the search for Brahma within oneself, and the identity of that inner self with the World-Soul who is present in every particle of the world, 'as butter is contained in cream',[3] yet the God of the Upanishads transcends the visible universe and is not merely identified with it: the idea of transcendence fluctuates, and rarely predominates, but it is there. He is 'The One spreader of the net, Who rules with His ruling powers. Who rules all the world with His ruling powers,'[4] He is the 'One embracer of the universe';[5] He 'stands like a tree established in Heaven'.[6]

---

[1] id. pp. 118–19, Brihad-Aranyaka Upanishad, 3, 8, 9–11 (with omissions).

[2] id. p. 360, Katha Upanishad, 6, 12.

[3] id. p. 397, Svetāsvarata Upanishad, 1, 16.

[4] id. p. 399, S.U., iii, 1.

[5] id. p. 407, S.U., v, 13.

[6] id. p. 400, S.U., iii, 9.

'The One, who, himself without colour, by the manifold application of his power,

'Distributes many colours in his hidden purpose, And into whom, its end and purpose, the whole world dissolves, —He is God. (deva).'[1] His power over temporal events is supreme, and He is a Person, to be known and adored.

Some sages discourse of inherent nature;
Others likewise of time. Deluded men!
It is the greatness of God in the world
By which this Brahma-wheel is caused to revolve.
He by whom the whole world is constantly enveloped,
Is intelligent, the author of time, the possessor of
  qualities, omniscient.
Ruled over by Him, His work revolves.[2]

Worship Him as the manifold, the origin of all being,
The adorable God who abides in one's own thoughts, the
  primaeval.
Higher and other than the world-tree, time, and forms,
Is He from whom this expanse proceeds.
The bringer of light, the remover of evil, the Lord of
  prosperity,
Know Him as in one's own self, as the immortal abode of all.
Him who is the supreme, mighty Lord of lords,
The supreme Divinity of divinities,
The supreme Ruler of rulers, paramount,
Him let us know as the adorable God, the Lord of the
  World.[3]

The date of Zarathustra, or Zoroaster, the Persian prophet and reformer, is uncertain, but is probably not

---

[1] id. p. 402, S.U., iv, 1.
[2] id. p. 408, S.U., vi, 1–2.
[3] id. p. 409, S.U., vi, 5–7.

later than 1000 B.C.; whatever of the Zoroastrian literature can be ascribed to Zarathustra himself or his immediate circle is therefore fully relevant, and the most ancient portions of the Zend-Avesta, the Gathas, are probably original and take us back to the mind and utterance of the prophet. There is, as one would expect, and in spite of marked variations, an evident kinship with the Vedic hymns. Ahura Mazda is in many respects identical with the Varuna of the Rig-Veda: there is the same wide outlook onto life and the same subordination of this vast universe to a sole Creator, in a spirit of wonder and awe.

'This I ask thee, O Ahura! tell me aright; Who by generation was the first father of the Righteous Order? Who gave the sun and stars their undeviating way? Who established that whereby the moon waxes, and whereby she wanes, save Thee? These things, O Great Creator, would I know, and others likewise still.

'This I ask Thee, O Ahura! tell me aright; who from beneath hath sustained the earth, and the clouds above, so that they do not fall? Who made the waters and the plants? Who to the wind has yoked on the storm-clouds...? Who, O great Creator, is the inspirer of the good thoughts within our souls?

'This I ask Thee, O Ahura! tell me aright: who, as a skilful artisan, hath made the lights and the darkness?...

'This I ask Thee, O Ahura! tell me aright these things which I shall speak forth, if they are truly thus. ... With questions such as these, so abundant, O Mazda! I press Thee, O bountiful Spirit, Thou maker of all!'[1]

The resemblance to the Varuna hymns of the Rig-Veda, and even to the earlier Upanishads, is very clear. But the religion of the Gathas is more fervent and individual, and

[1] *Sacred Books of the East*, vol. xxxi (Oxford, 1887). The Zend-Avesta, Part III, pp. 112–15. The Gathas, Yasna XLIV, 3–7 (with omissions).

stamped with the character of a personal experience. The dualism of their outlook, which has been said to vitiate any true monotheism in Zoroastrian religion, is perhaps rather the intense dramatic expression of Zarathustra's own sense of evil as a power to be fought, than a logically conceived dualism of an equal and eternal Light and Darkness. The reader of the Gathas feels that Ahura Mazda is supreme, less, as it were, by quantitative authority than by the quality of his power, at once searching and harmonizing, which orders and integrates the universe by its penetration in a way which evil is powerless to do.

'Therefore as the first did I conceive of Thee, O Ahura Mazda! as the one to be adored with the mind in the creation, as the Father of the Good Mind within us, when I beheld Thee with my eyes as the veritable maker of our righteousness, as the Lord of the actions of life.'[1]

The conception of 'orderliness' produced by 'piety', so that the 'good mind' in man may correspond with the 'Good Mind' in Ahura, is perhaps the most valuable element in the Gathas. Though the expression of it is often so close and compressed as to be obscure, it seems to grow naturally out of a personal religious experience of great delicacy and constancy, persisting over a number of years. The Upanishads provide an early and beautiful example of religious thought: the Gathas balance this by exhibiting the shaping and refining influence of religious experience on an individual mind.

Persian religion, and something of Zarathustra's life and teaching, were known to the Greeks as early as Herodotus. But Greek religion is a more complex manifold than that of either Persia or India, owing partly to the mixed character of the Greek race, and partly to their contacts over a very long period with both Asia and Egypt.

[1] id. p. 44, Yasna XXXI, 8.

THE DISPENSATION OF PAGANISM

The gods of Olympus recognizably derive from the Indo-European nature-gods, though a more sophisticated mythology has emptied them of much of their real significance for worship. But there were deeper undercurrents of religious life in Greece, seeking both intimate communion with the god and the purification, in more than a ceremonial sense, of the individual. These hopes and desires found their outlet in the Greek mystery cults which doubtless owed much to Egypt. But their sources may lie still farther back, in a period older than the descent of the Aryan race into the Mediterranean, and we are here perhaps in contact with the very oldest element in the composition of Greek religious thought. This complexity of origin had many valuable results. When the early thinkers of Greece outgrew the mythology of Olympus, they developed easily and naturally the idea of close communion between the individual soul and the Divine power, and of purification as the means by which communion could be assured; yet the strong and simple influence of Olympian worship retained transcendence and authority as Divine characteristics, and prevented the drift of Greek thought towards a Pantheism in which God and the world are identical and the aim of purification is the dissolution of the self into the Divine Whole. There was a tendency in this direction among some early Greek thinkers, which reasserted itself much later in Stoicism, but as a whole it was mastered and outgrown; and this power of holding together contrasting elements in coherence helped to give its special balance and richness and intellectual dignity to the mature religious thought of Greece. Historically it is possible to see how the great work of Socrates and Plato was directed and influenced in three ways; by the philosophy of creation which had occupied early thinkers among the Greeks, just as in India and Persia; by the intimate self-purification taught in Orphism, which Pythagoras had utilized, divested it of its cruder ceremonial elements, and given a permanently ethical character; most important of all, by the conception of purification as leading to vision, a conception which characterized Orphism, however dimly and crudely the object of vision was conceived. It was natural, therefore, that clearer and fuller ideas of the ultimate Object of vision should accompany this process of fusion. Such conceptions are illustrated in the quotations which follow, and they deserve our close attention. Not only are the conceptions great and lofty in themselves but they are grasped and defined with a firmness and lucidity altogether new: we seem to be entering a new spiritual climate and atmosphere, and to be advancing upward into the purest and clearest of mountain air.

It would be wrong to say that there is no true religious feeling in Homer, and the transcendence of Zeus made it easy for the Greek thinkers of the sixth and fifth centuries, when they discarded the polytheism of Homer and Hesiod, to develop the idea of unity in the Godhead. But the main trend of their thought was towards unity rather than either personality or transcendence. They often retained and used the name of Zeus, but with a premise of its inadequacy to convey any true idea. This is the probable meaning of the enigmatic saying of Heraclitus: ‘ἕν τὸ σοφὸν μοῦνον λέγεσθαι ἐθέλει καὶ οὐκ ἐθέλει, Ζηνὸς ὄνομα,——’[1] ‘One thing alone the Wise wills and wills not to be called —the name of Zeus’; and the thought recurs, though with a more positive content, in Aeschylus. ‘Zeus—Whoever he is, if this it is his pleasure to be called, this name I call him.’[2] The Unity of God, and His Otherness than man, are strongly emphasized in the celebrated fragment of Xenophanes, but it is at least possible that his

[1] Fr. 65.   [2] Aeschylus, *Agamemnon*, ll. 160–2.

31

θεός is to be identified with the visible universe: and if so, early Greek thought, here as elsewhere, touches the Pantheism of the Upanishads. Εἷς θεὸς ἔν τε θεοῖσι καὶ νἀθρώποισι μέγιστος, οὔτε δέμας θνητοῖσιν ὁμοίιος, οὔτε νόημα. 'There is one God, greatest among both gods and men, like to mortals neither in form nor in thought.'[1] The One Being of Parmenides, 'indestructible, entire, unshakable',[2] was apparently material and identical with the world: and the preoccupation of early Greek philosophy with the substance of Being, and not with its ethical or spiritual character, was bound to lead either to Pantheism or to Atheism, however pure and refined and remote from the apprehension of the senses the underlying stuff of all things was considered to be. It was no wonder that all the variety and vitality of early Greek thought threatened to dissolve in scepticism: and it was the life work of Socrates, under the most urgent sense of a divine vocation, to rescue this unparalleled mental life from such an annihilation and to place it on firm ground. Socrates was not concerned with theology in the narrower sense: it was part of his vocation to receive the Divine guidance which had come to him, through the accepted religious forms from the oracle at Delphi, no less obediently than the guidance which had visited him personally through his own experience of a Divine voice within. But his especial concern was to maintain the real existence of unchangeable Truth and the possibility of its apprehension by all those who would give themselves up to seek it in complete humility and single-mindedness. His work, however negative and partial, was to develop a method through which the human reason, stripped of prejudice and self-seeking, and deeply concerned with the soul's betterment, could place itself in a right relationship to Truth. The words which Plato

[1] Fr. 1.   [2] Parmenides, ll. 59–60.

ascribes to him in the Apology, even if not verbally exact, are a faithful presentation of his method and aim.

'Men of Athens, I honour and love you, but I shall obey the God rather than you, and as long as I breathe, and have the power, never shall I cease my pursuit and love of wisdom, and my exhortation of you, and my exposition of truth to whomsoever I meet, saying in my accustomed manner: "Good friend, you are an Athenian, of a city so great and famous in wisdom and strength; and are you not ashamed to take so much thought for wealth, that you may have as much as is possible, and for repute and honour, while for wisdom, and strength, and for your own soul, that it may be as good as is possible, you take no thought nor care? And if any one of you gainsays me and maintains that he does so care, I will not let him go or depart from him, but I shall question and cross-question and cross-examine him, and if I think that he has not virtue though he declare that he has, I shall reproach him, because he sets least value on what is worthy of most, and upon what is less worthy he sets more. This I shall do to young or old, to anyone that I meet, be he stranger or citizen, but to my fellow-citizens by preference as they are nearer to me in blood. For this the God commands me, know it well, and I believe that no greater good has yet happened to you in the city than my service to the God." '[1]

Using this method of critical analysis for the purgation of the intellect from superficial opinions and motives, Plato proceeded to build the Theory of Ideas; of the real existence, that is, of universal qualities from which particulars derive their identity and character, and to which they only inadequately correspond. The Ideas of Plato are not vague abstractions, but firm and transparent as diamond; they are far more real in their strength and sub-

---

[1] Plato, *Apology*, 29d–30a.

stantial character than the concrete and individualized world which derives from them, and they represent the complete victory of Greek thought over any temptation to limit reality by the material universe. The Platonic Theory of Ideas has received much criticism, from Aristotle onwards, and it is not Plato's own last word; but perhaps language has never said more clearly than with this golden voice of Athens:

My soul, there is a country
Far beyond the stars.

'But the region above the heaven—no poet of those here on earth ever yet sang of it worthily, nor ever shall. But it is something like this. For I must boldly attempt to tell the truth, especially since truth is my theme. For real essential being, without colour, without form, intangible, visible only to thought which is the pilot of the soul, being which is the object of true knowledge, is the dweller in this place. Thus the intelligence of a god, inasmuch as it is nurtured on thought and knowledge undefiled, and the intelligence of every soul which cares to receive its right spiritual food, beholding true being for a long space of time, is satisfied with it, and, gazing upon the truth, is nourished and made glad, until the revolution in its cycle carries it round into the same place again. In the revolution it beholds absolute Justice, Temperance, Knowledge —not the knowledge which has a beginning and which is a varied kind of knowledge associated with the various things which we now call realities, but the knowledge which abides in that which really and truly is; and when the soul has gazed in like manner upon the rest of the truly existent realities and has feasted upon them, it descends again into the interior of the heaven and goes home.'[1]

[1] Plato, *Phaedrus*, 247c–e.

34

This passage from the myth of the Charioteer is followed by the description of reminiscence, in which Plato dwells naturally upon the contrast between the scarcely remembered realities 'yonder', and the copies 'here'.

'Every human soul has by its nature gazed upon the realities, or it would not have entered into this human form, but to remember the realities yonder from the copies here on earth is not easy for every soul—neither for those who then for a short space beheld the things above, nor for those who on falling to earth so miscarried that by evil communications they turned to unrighteousness and forgot the holy things which they once beheld. A few souls indeed are left in whom the power of reminiscence is still sufficiently alive. These, whenever they see some likeness of the realities yonder, are astounded, and no longer masters of themselves, but what ails them they know not, because their perception is not sufficient and complete. Now of justice, and temperance, and all else that is precious to souls, there is no beam at all in the copies here below, but because of the dullness of our organs only a few of mankind, when they approach the images, behold the nature of that which is imaged there.'[1]

Closely associated with these is the description of pure Beauty as the object of vision in the 'Symposium'. ' "What do we think, then," she said, "if it were any man's fortune to behold the absolute Beauty, uncorrupted, pure, and uncommingled, not beauty contaminated by human flesh and colour and much other mortal worthlessness—no, but if he could see the Divine loveliness itself, in sole simplicity of form? Do you think," she said, "that such a life would be paltry, looking thither?" '[2]

These passages are not only the epitome of Platonic idealism, but hold an unrivalled place in Greek religious

[1] id. 249e–250b.   [2] *Symposium*, 211e–212a.

literature from the depth and spontaneity of personal experience which they convey. But there is a unification of thought in his later writings, an increased concentration on the Idea of the one Good into whose nature the other qualities must enter. In the 'Philebus' he dwells, though briefly, on this Supreme Idea of the Good, in which the other ideas subsist, so that the Good is a complex existence of Beauty, Truth and Symmetry: and it is the infusion of this complex identity which is the cause of the goodness in each created thing. In the latest dialogues, the idea of Cause predominates, and the Good is regarded as generating and purposive activity, possessing movement and life and thought. 'Can we,' asks the unnamed Eleatic visitor in the 'Sophist', 'Can we be readily brought to believe that motion and life and soul and thought are not present in Absolute Being?—Can we believe that Being does not live and does not think, but is a venerable, holy, mindless thing, static and motionless?'[1] These words may be dramatically appropriate to the speaker: but the purposive and creative character of Eternal Being is consistently maintained, both in the mythology of the Timaeus and with great dignity and gravity by the Athenian speaker in the Laws.

The Divine Being thus conceived does not work in detachment and indifference, but has claims on man and a deep interest in his betterment: His chief claim is that men should aspire to the very best and highest in every sphere of life, and thus grow like God Himself and partake of the Divine nature and immortality. This can be illustrated again and again in Plato, and its fullest exposition, in the Fourth and Tenth Books of the Laws, though cast in the accepted forms of contemporary Greek religion, is consistent with the whole tenor of his faith: it would be

---

[1] *Sophist*, 248e–249a.

incompatible with the character of perfect Being not to make the highest demands on man. 'There must be likeness to God as far as possible';[1] righteousness, holiness and wisdom are both the means and the condition of this likeness.

Yet the clearest and fullest picture of the Divine Life which pre-Christian thought has to give us, is found, not in Plato, but in the great twelfth book of Aristotle's Metaphysics. The life of God is the unbroken happiness of pure contemplation, in which entire perfection knows and beholds entire perfection, which is Itself: and this contemplation is activity and reality in their intensest form. 'And life belongs to God: for the actuality of thought is life, and God is that actuality: and the essential actuality of God is life, the best life, and everlasting. We affirm then that God is a living being, everlasting, best, so that life, and continuous, everlasting duration, belong to God: for this is what God is.'[2] Taken from their context of close reasoning, these words are very simple, and they read even more simply in Greek: but it is that inspired simplicity by which Aristotle seems often to reach the very heart of his subject, whatever the subject may be, and whether he is dealing with the structure of the lowest forms of life or with the depth of the Divine Nature, to leave his readers feeling that he has spoken the right and inevitable word.

It is often said that Aristotle's Supreme Being, whose whole knowledge is self-knowledge and who moves the world solely because He is its object of desire, is detached and indifferent to humanity: but this is not necessarily so. The Divine Activity is the source of every other activity that there is, simply and purely by Its own Supreme attractiveness: the Divine Life is always wholly, fully and un-

[1] *Theaetetus*, 176b.
[2] Aristotle, *Metaphysics*, 1072b.

changeably, that best life which man experiences fitfully and partially: man's happiness lies in increasing those moments of joy by every means in his power, and so becoming like to God. Aristotle never discusses the far-reaching implications of these sayings, particularly as to the Nature of that Being whose supreme desirableness is the motive principle of the universe. They are like the flashes of brilliant intuition by which a great scientific discovery or mathematical proof crowns years of labour and calculation, and (while seeming to come suddenly from nowhere) is the reward of much apparently fruitless work. In the same way these touches of inspiration and insight into the Being of God Himself are the crown of the life-work of Aristotle, and the undeveloped and almost casual way in which they are set down disguised a vast potentiality for the future.

It is legitimate to consider these developments in some detail, for they form a very important chapter in the history of religious thought. Their importance has sometimes been obscured by their lack of emphasis on the personal: these great apprehensions of reality at which the Greeks arrived are concerned with Goodness and Beauty and Truth in their abstract and universal character, with τὰ ὄντα rather than with ὁ ὤν: even the One Good which crowns the hierarchy of universals, though freely described as θεός, is not yet in any recognizable sense a Personal God. But this is not a disadvantage: it is the essence of the Greek 'revelation'—to anticipate for a moment in using the term—that it was concerned with eternal qualities and modes of being, and thus provided a wide and deep expanse in which, eventually, an enlarged conception of Divine Personality could freely grow and develop. It was in fact the especial task of the Greek religious genius to discard utterly the persistent anthropomorphism of its own religion, and by its preoccupation with the universal and eternal, and its searching definition of qualities, to prepare the way for a deeper and truer understanding of the nature of Person, and its relation to the Being of God.

Chapter Three

THE MARKS OF UNIVERSALITY
IN RELIGION

We have shifted our centre for the time being from Jerusalem as the cradle of Christianity and the heart and focus of comparative religion; let us carry this change of view-point further still. Imagine an intelligent being from another planet, looking with a wide view on to our Earth, over the three thousand years before the birth of Christ. What he would see might be pictured as a great plain, from which mountain ridges and peaks emerged at intervals, loosely united in a single system, and of very varying configuration, height, and grandeur: some of a deep and dazzling brightness, others with their outline obscured by forestation, or concealed in mist: but all united by a link of structural unity at times clearly visible in bare rock. This unity underlying all variation might not unjustly be described as belief in God: in God as ruler and Transcendent: in God as Creator, as Holy and as Righteous: and in God as requiring some kind of righteousness and holiness in man. Were this observer to be entirely devoid of all religious belief and experience, yet quite unprejudiced as to its probability, he could reasonably conclude, without ceasing to be in a true sense 'agnostic', that the uncaused cause of this unity of experience was the real Existence of God.

This widespread sense of a Divine Being, and grasp of His Goodness, might be thought to give the religious intuition all its necessary scope and aim: yet where this sense was at its finest and most delicate it was accompanied, not by the deep repose and satisfaction with which the mind rests upon ultimate mystery, but by dissatisfaction and consciousness of incompleteness. 'The Maker and Father of this universe is hard to find.'[1] The best conclusions of human thought were felt to be slight and provisional, a 'raft'[2] for the voyage of life: only the assurance of a 'divine word'[2] could ratify them. This awareness that the hopes of God and of immortality rested on an inadequate foundation, which we find especially in Plato, was itself a valuable contribution: it was negative evidence for the possibilities of 'depths beyond depths', at present beyond human apprehension, but not necessarily so for ever. But the great intellectual conceptions of God lacked finality, also, in a very different way. They failed altogether to penetrate, or absorb into themselves, existing religious practice or traditions, and all the deeply-rooted ideas of sacrifice, oracular communications, and omens. This physical and material view of religion continued side by side with the growth of abstract thought about the Divine Being, and it is not enough merely to say that it represented a less worthy idea of Him which it was necessary to outgrow. On the contrary, these crude superstitions and beliefs often contained profound religious truths. In the two aspects of sacrifice, the propitiation and the nourishment of the god, lie the germ of two great ideas, that man has in some way sinned and become displeasing to God, and yet that God wills to use everything that man can give, for His own service and purposes. The whole conception of sacrifice and the sacrificial meal, and of oracular revelations, foreshadow truths of the deepest religious importance, that God wills to enter into the most

[1] Plato, *Timaeus*, 28c.   [2] *Phaedo*, 85c–d.

intimate and familiar relations with His creature Man, and that He wills to speak to him. Taken as a whole, the common stock of everyday superstition and observance perhaps contained elements even more vital and indispensable to religious life than the sublime poetry and thought which grew out of them and away from them without full acknowledgement of its origin. They teach us, that to be truly inclusive and universal, religion must be in the closest association with everyday life, and that in the last resort it cannot depend on the purely rational faculty. It must strike deep down into the roots of human nature, and operate, for good or evil, in that world of instinctive choices, needs, and reactions, of which man is rationally unaware, but which expresses itself in the language of folk-tale, myth and ritual, all over the world. Moreover, in this tangled forestation of primitive worship, where human hopes and desires are seen in complex interplay and strange elaboration of expression, we approach nearer than before to what seems like a real consciousness of the supernatural: belief in the reality of some kind of action from the Divine side lies at the heart of every ceremonial, and is the fundamental reason for its performance.

But it is noteworthy that in the very places where the conception of the Divine Nature reached its most wonderful levels, the spiritual life and practice of everyday religion remained comparatively low. The idol-worship of Hinduism, the anthropomorphic polytheism of Greece, Roman enslavement to omens, and to crude, cruel methods of propitiation, all point the same direction. There was cleavage, deep and wide, between the commonly accepted beliefs and practices of the mass of the people, and those of an enlightened few. The great religious thought which we have been studying lacked universal character in its own highest development: it was confessedly the prerogative of a few, and these few accepted and acquiesced in the religion of the common people as a necessary mythology, because they believed true ideas to be beyond the understanding of most men.

These conclusions might be summarized as follows: The conception of God formed by pre-Christian thought outside Palestine included His Unity, His Eternal Being, His creating Power, His Holiness, His claim upon men that they should live well. But such a conception was the privilege of a few only, and the general level of thought and worship was lower: it was crudely polytheistic, full of primitive superstitions, childish in its credulity and with a merely magical view of prayer and sacrifice: there was often little perception of a necessary link between religion and good life. Yet these crude religious ideas had something which the higher lacked, a vivid sense of intimate contact and communion between man and the supernatural, and of an activity towards man proceeding from the Beings worshipped; and they were universal in their absence of exclusiveness and their wide availability for all. A truly universal religion, could such exist, would gather together these differing elements into one, and would unite, inseparably, true apprehensions of God's Nature with a true awareness about His activity towards man: no conceptual apprehension—however fully grasped and formulated by the intellect—which had failed to absorb and refine the sensuous and perceptive element in religious experience, could have ultimate and authoritative character. But this power of absorption and re-interpretation must go beyond what is specifically religious: if there is any one characteristic which is indispensable to a universal religion, it is the power to utilize every vestige of human capacity without suppression or mutilation. What radical transforming, or what deeper elucidation of human

43

nature, will be the result of such utilization, is a further question: but the first condition of universality in religion is that nothing be left unpermeated and ignored: religion must be vitally related to the whole of human nature and experience, and not only to its intellectual part. A second condition must be universal availability; and this implies both an inexhaustible depth of intellectual content, and a simplicity of character which will bring the innermost and deepest truths of religion within the apprehension of all. They must be capable of being known with a knowledge which, though necessarily inadequate, is yet true as far as it goes. Degrees of apprehension may vary, and an element of superstition will often be present, but the simplest and least educated mind must be capable of knowing and understanding the fundamentals of faith. Depth and lucidity and simplicity are qualities which we should anticipate and desire in a religion which is ultimately to satisfy the whole need of men.

We can thus form a conception of what universality in religion might mean; yet the consideration of what is implied by universality in other fields may take us farther. The consciousness of space and time, and the conceptions of number and relation, are universal elements in our experience, and they have certain characteristics in common. The first is that they are fundamentally mysterious and have to be taken for granted; next that they are permanent; then that in spite of their mysterious character, they are felt to be clear and simple; lastly, that they are continuously supported and confirmed by the evidence of experience. They are not only a part of our consciousness, but a usable and effective part: not only our mental enrichment, but the instruments of our daily life. These marks of universality in other fields might be expressed as mystery, simplicity, permanence, and an unbroken accord with experience

44

which gives them dependableness and practical value.

But these 'universals' of ordinary experience have something further in common, implicit no doubt in what has already been said, and of even greater significance. They are felt to exist, in some sense, externally to ourselves, or rather to represent to us, in forms determined by no choice of our own, but by the nature of human consciousness, something which does so exist. We do not arrive at them through the sum total of our observations, but we possess them as 'given' elements, we defer to them as inescapably authoritative, and we use them to interpret our whole material and mental environment. Further, we treat these 'given' elements in our consciousness as in some sense, indefinitely applicable, and of wider extension than the particulars which they interpret, just as a child's latent power to walk extends beyond the first actual movements of its limbs.

To apply the same criterion of universality to religion may seem at first sight to be a hazardous analogy. Yet if the religious consciousness is a real part of man's nature, possessed by all even though latent in some, it may be expected to share the character of whatever else is universal and necessary to our existence: and in fact there are signs that it does. We recognize the same characters of mystery and simplicity in an inseparable combination; of persistence and indestructibility, and practical correspondence with experience: and its validity, which is felt to be unquestionable, depends upon the conviction that it is not deduced from experience, but is the representative form of a prior reality. It is in virtue of this objective character that it is felt to extend, not only beyond the religious experience of each individual, but beyond the sum total of the religious experiences of all individuals that it is possible to conceive. It represents in fact, like our other *a priori* intuitions and conceptions, an infinite reality, infinitely applicable, though the form in which we apprehend that reality may be indefinitely capable of difference; there may exist rational beings whose consciousness is unlike ours, or, in a future state, the form of our own apprehension may be unlike what it is now. The difference between the religious consciousness and the rest of our *a priori* knowledge lies not in its character, but in the field of its operation. It ranges far beyond the borders of what can be seen or conceived, and occupies itself with an object which is not fully exhibited to it either by the senses or by the intellect. It insists on regarding this Divine object as a firm and unchallengeable certainty: yet this sense of certainty is as little a disturbance of normality in those who possess it as is their certainty of time or number. Here, perhaps, despite its apparent wide variation in individuals, is genuine evidence for its validity. All our intuitive and self-evident knowledge is characterized by healthful certainty, and it is doubtful whether any other part of our knowledge is. If for no other reason, there would seem some real ground here for placing the religious intuition within the category of 'universals'—as belonging, that is, to the part of our knowledge which is intuitive, self-evident, and *a priori*.

But where this certainty is applied to something so remote and startling as metaphysical existence, our reason requires that it be justified, like everything else which we consider real, by evidence within our experience. Our intuitive grasp of our other certainties, of space and time, of number, distinction, and relation, is continually being confirmed, in one way and another, by our environment, and this perpetual interaction of knowledge and experience makes the sum total of our daily life. We may justly demand that the religious consciousness should meet with the same experimental confirmation: if it failed to do so, we should be bound to regard it as a mere, though strong, survival from the primitive stages of life, and it would be our duty, however difficult, to discard it. Such confirmation must be widespread and of substantial uniformity. A merely individual sense of accord will be no more conclusive here than elsewhere, and only a vast unity of experience can provide the required justification. Moreover in the case of the religious consciousness, even the most impressive unity of personal experience cannot alone suffice: there must be evidence worth weighing, from the Godward side, that the world of supernatural reality exists, and that through the knowledge and worship and desire of which the religious consciousness is blended, humanity strikes deep roots into that other world. If this second, more external type of evidence were lacking we could at best but regard our religious sense as a mythological expression of humanity's highest ideals, and strive to rewrite it in terms applicable to a more informed psychology. Thus the empirical confirmation for which we are looking will be of two rather different kinds. It will consist of evidence for the coherent and substantially uniform effect upon individuals of their personal religious experience and evidence for the coherent and self-consistent action of God in the process of history.

A very simple illustration will make the two types of evidence clearer. Each of us who possesses sight is conscious, as an individual, of objects presented to his vision—a mountain, let us say, or a ploughed field. He is aware that, approximately at any rate, the same objects are visible to others, and his belief in the reality of the object is partly derived from this visual identity. But he realizes that this alone is not sufficient evidence for the existence of field and mountain externally to himself and others, though it is cumulative evidence, tantamount to proof, for the uniform tendency of the mind to form such images, so that they may be said to exist at any rate within human minds: and if he experienced nothing from the objects seen except the sight of them, there the matter must rest. But they exhibit a powerful tendency to influence him in far different ways: the mountain, in volcano or avalanche, may be the cause of widespread ruin and dissolution to himself and others of the human family: the field, which he has himself ploughed, he knows to be the source of the nourishment on which his own life and that of his fellows depend, and he knows that without such nourishment his life will wither and sink back into that very earth of the field. It is by evidence such as this, age-long and invariable, that he is profoundly persuaded of exterior life and reality in the objects presented to his eyes.

There must be these same two factors in whatever exists and is known; our own knowledge of it, and an effect upon ourselves which would take place even apart from our knowledge and which operates in entire independence: where these factors are present we habitually conclude existence. The required complement of our personal experience, in the field of religion, is action from the Divine side, action both effectual and indispensable to us for life and power. This action, if we are to know it at all, must operate immediately in our world of space and time, though it may reach out far beyond them in its results: it will therefore be a visible and apprehensible action of God in history. This self-disclosure of God through evidenced action is what we call revelation; and Revelation is thus the 'articulation'[1] of a Reality which would otherwise be in-

---

[1] The word was suggested, I think, by a passage in *Introduction to Dogmatic Theology*, Rev. F. J. Hall, D.P., chapter ii, p. 53: 'More articulate revelations, such as will authenticate and define Nature's teaching.'

communicable to humanity in decipherable terms: the symbolic disclosures of Nature, however mysteriously suggestive of a hidden Power and Beauty, can never be other than enigmatic in themselves. It follows that any religion which is to have permanent claims on faith must have this evidential and historical element, or it will always lie under suspicion of being purely subjective. But the revelation of God must be much more than a token: it must have the same momentous character for our spiritual life as the great realities of Nature have for our life in the material world. It must, that is, show God as acting prior to either our knowledge or our response, and ourselves as completely dependent for the growth and maintenance of our religious life upon such prior action.

This investigation of universality in our other experience has carried us a considerable way, and has strengthened the hypothesis that the religious consciousness is a part of our fundamental equipment for life, and is therefore indispensable to the full development of our faculties and the fullest correspondence with our environment. It is no real objection that in some the religious sense appears to be entirely obscured throughout their whole lives, that it is always very variable as between individuals, and that under the more artificial conditions of modern life it seems readily obscured: for this is true, and in some cases markedly true, of our primary intuitions and perceptions in other fields. But all 'given' knowledge presupposes what is exterior to ourselves, the proof of which comes home to us in various ways according to the nature of what is experienced: and the external proof for religious experience —proof up to such limit of probability as the limits of human perceptions allow—lies in well-evidenced revelation. A serious examination of the revealed element in any religion is indispensable for all who would judge its truth:

and where a high degree of well-attested revelation co-
exists with wide and deep uniformity of experience, there
are the stronger grounds for faith. Thus religious experience conforms to the same tests of existence and objec-
tivity as the rest of our experience, and a religion is of
highest value where such correspondence is most complete.

Yet in the great religious thought and experience which
we have so far considered, whether of India, Persia, or
Greece, this historical and evidential character is lacking.
The mind, the emotions, the imagination are at work, but
there is no really adequate evidence for that Other whom
they presuppose. The deep devotion shown, whether in
Orphism towards Dionysos, in Hinduism towards
Brahma, in Plato towards the Supreme Good, however
impressive and beautiful, is evidence of subjective experience only: the objects of love are either simply mythological, or, as in Plato, are the logical climax of a chain of
human reasoning and can therefore only amount to a
probability. We seemed closest to a direct consciousness of
supernatural Reality in the most crude and primitive parts
of ancient religion: but all was confused and unsubstan-
tiated by any true responsive evidence.

When we turn back at last to Palestine and to the religious experience of the Jews, we are conscious of difference and even contrast, in spite of much that is the
same. We find the same crudity in the earliest stages of
development, and we find, just as in other religions, individuals whose vision of God appears wider and deeper
than that of their contemporaries, and who influence and
purify the common thought and practice, in varying degrees and at different times: the work of Isaiah is not
essentially different in this from that of Zarathustra or
Socrates. In these ways Jewish religion only exhibits, al-

though pre-eminently, the normal characteristics of all religious growth, and it might be thought to reach its own highest point by a natural process in Christianity, where the cruder morality and ritual taboos of the Mosaic Law are given a new interpretation and direction by the potent influence of its Founder: there could be no reason from this point of view, why Christianity should not be further developed and refined in its turn by the influence of others. Thus regarded, Jewish religion presents no contrast, and has no unique importance except for the great genius of its individuals.

But the special character of Judaism is really very different: it lies in its claim to present a record of Divine action, manifested in space and time and controlling the whole course of history. This is not simply stated as a general truth, in the sense in which Zeus may be said to govern the world, or Brahma to be omnipresent in it, but exhibited in full detail through a whole varied literature, extending over centuries. The value of this literature as a record of event varies greatly: in places it has no strict significance as fact, and it leaves room for controversy everywhere. Yet when the Old and New Testaments are taken together, they certainly provide a most important body of evidence for the view that a guiding Activity, greater than that of man, was present throughout, that the meaning and intention of His Action can be to some extent understood, and that a main part of the Action was the deliberate revelation of the Nature which underlay that purpose and meaning. Jewish religion thus makes a powerful claim to provide that second type of evidence, which we have seen to be needed as the complement of inner experience in every sphere of knowledge—evidence for the existence, in some sense externally to the subject, of the object known. Whatever else we find in Christianity and its great Forerunner, we shall find this certainly, that it purports, more than other religions, to be an intelligible and historical self-disclosure of God to man. The religion of Palestine stands at the bar of History, claiming to authenticate by its testimony that sense of overshadowing Power and Existence which has been with man from the beginning: claiming to confirm transcendently that interior witness by which prophets of all races and ages have spoken wonderfully of the Divine. The reasonable establishment of this claim is not a rhetorical, but in the deepest and truest sense a philosophical victory: it is here, rather than in the beauty or novelty of its teaching, that the profession of Christianity to have universal significance will find its first ground.

Chapter Four

THE REDEMPTIVE CHARACTER
OF CHRISTIANITY

The universal claim of Christianity is derived in the first instance from its historical character: it purports to be the climax of a divine revelation, such as in fullness, development, and consistency is found nowhere else, and to rest its claim upon a varied testimony which the severest cross-examinations of historical criticism have been unable to break down. Yet, vital and indispensable as this time-character is, it is not by itself sufficient: it must still be shown that the content of the revelation is truly universal, so that the whole nature of every man, irrespective of race, or class, or colour, is more deeply integrated and harmonized by acceptance of its truth than by any other means. This, in fact, is the vast and daring claim of the followers of Jesus, and has been so from the beginning: and it calls forth, now as at the first, natural and prompt rejection.

This rejection seems even more reasonable now than then, for the Christian Church now faces the world with a long life of frailty and error behind it: if the lives of Christian people are said to be often even less fully harmonized than those of others, the protest, in many cases, is obviously true. Yet though this is a real and great stumbling-block, so great as to be practically insuperable for many minds, our most careful thinking shows that it is not a fundamental objection. The degree to which individuals realize the full implications of their faith varies in depth and clearness; the decision and whole-heartedness with which they submit themselves to be penetrated and transformed by their belief varies even more; and this is even truer and therefore more conspicuous in the social than in the individual sphere of religion. Thus what the outer world normally sees, in a company of professing Christians, is a body whose members are all more or less imperfectly penetrated by the truths which they do in sincerity believe. The hindrances to fuller penetration are usually both moral and intellectual; defects in knowledge and understanding, sometimes too deeply ingrained to be removable, and sluggishness of desire and will. The criticism and condemnation which such a condition evokes may be too bitter, but is not unjust. Yet the condition itself is an imperfection of fact; it is not a limitation of possibility.

But there is a further objection which is felt by many just and sincere minds, and it is one which is deeper and more difficult to answer. A revelation might be of Divine origin, and true, without being universally intended. Christianity could thus be capable of very wide extension and yet ultimately find the limits of its applicability. It might be intended to command the allegiance of certain races and to be, for them, the final Word of God: if so, it is by an arbitrary presumption that they seek to extend it further, and they should humbly apply words written in another sense to their own small spiritual universe:

> There may be other Words for other worlds,
> But for this world, the Word of God is Christ.

It may at once be allowed that such localized revelations do, in all probability, exist, and are true self-disclosures of God, but are limited in their purpose. They may be revelations given to an individual, to empower him for a special task, or given in order to raise some one nation or community to a higher level of life and thought, that it may be the nucleus and centre of some purposed good for the surrounding races, or for humanity as a whole. The 'divine voice' of Socrates would be an example of the first, and such an experience as that of Zarathustra of the second. The influence of such revelations is indeed immeasurable, but their content is limited, in its fullness of meaning, to the time and place of their occurrence: they are valid, but they are not universal. If the revelation of God in Christ differs from these, it must differ essentially, and it is on this difference that its universal character depends. We are thus brought back to the need for a careful scrutiny of the Christian revelation, and a consideration of what appeared to be its essentials in the mind of Christ Himself and His immediate followers. From this we must eventually look back, retrace our argument, and consider how far these essentials conform to those characteristics of universality which suggested themselves to our quiet unbiassed thinking.

There are three scenes in the New Testament which have a bearing on this question and which help us to approach it in the right frame of mind. In studying them it is with no sense of authoritative character, for at this stage of inquiry no authority can be assumed; but they indicate something either of the mind and outlook of Christ, as mirrored and interpreted by his immediate followers, or of the outlook of those who collected and recorded the narratives.

The first is the Epiphany, whose festival sub-title in our Calendar, the Manifestation of Christ to the Gentiles, indicates the symbolic meaning which accompanies the story. The high and adventurous wisdom of other races and especially races of the East, here follows the Star and finds the Cradle and offers up its gifts of adoration and self-abnegating love. Here, beautifully symbolized, is the revelation of God to other races, a revelation at once partial and true, and also the universal, God-given attraction of the Babe. The story sanctions all the bold and deep reaches of man's quest for Truth, and thus unites Christianity from the very beginning with the sanctification, not suppression, of the intellect: yet it places all human search and knowledge in a unique attitude of adoration and self-giving towards the Human Person of Jesus. The symbol is capable of unbounded application; and it is, at least, significant and relevant, on the threshold of a search for the unique, and yet universal, in Christianity.

The second, the Transfiguration of our Lord, is more firmly rooted in history; the accounts of it, especially perhaps that of St. Luke, bear marks of coming from an eye-witness, and the withdrawal for prayer by which it was preceded was marked by Jesus Himself with peculiar importance and intimacy. The three disciples whom He chose to accompany Him to this mountain-top were those who were admitted into the room where Jairus's little daughter lay, and those whom He took with Him into the Garden of His Agony; they were those, evidently, whom He desired to have with Him, for whatever reason, in some of the most profound and costly experiences of His Life on earth. In this case it seems clear that a truth of vast importance was left impressed upon their minds, though its full depth and range could only be understood gradually. Their first conception of the three figures of the Vision was of three who were equals in importance. 'Let us make three tabernacles.' But as soon as Peter had spoken he felt that the words were inadequate to the facts, and that he had spoken 'without knowing what he said'. The Voice which followed the vision brought this home to the disciples' consciousness. 'This is My Son, my Chosen apart,' as is the version of St. Luke. The disciples shared, at the Transfiguration, the knowledge which Jesus had of His unique Sonship, and thus received in its germ the revelation of what we describe as the Divinity of Christ. This knowledge was not realized by them, if indeed it ever can be, in terms of mental grasp and formal assent. They had ascended the mountain with a knowledge of Jesus as Prophet, Teacher, and Healer, which had already led one at least of them to acknowledge Him as the expected Messiah, and in that sense Son of God. They descended it, one would venture to say, with little sense of any formal change in their view, but with the confused impress of an experience which would only very gradually express itself in their conscious lives. 'Majesty, power, and glory' are the words (due possibly to St. Peter)[1] in which this experience was later adumbrated. Like the Epiphany, the Transfiguration isolates the Human Person of Jesus and subordinates all preconceptions in a free and voluntary submissiveness.

The third incident is the request of 'the Greeks' to see Jesus, a few days only before His death. Recorded for us by St. John in a passage of great depth and importance,[2] it may reveal a little to us of our Lord's own mind during the last days of His life on earth: His awareness of the vast scope of His mission, His longing love for souls, yet His complete knowledge that He could only reach them through the door of His Death. 'Except a grain of wheat fall into the earth and die, it abideth by itself alone: but if it die, it bringeth forth much fruit.' It would appear that the request was not granted: 'He departed and hid Himself.' But the universal scope of His mission to the world, which was to begin at His Death, is emphasized with great

[1] 2 Peter i, 16, 17.   [2] St. John xii, 20–36.

solemnity. The whole episode seems to be a sequel to the Baptism and the Transfiguration, and to complete the isolation of Jesus for a unique mission, while it exhibits more fully than ever before, its sacrificial and saving character. Each of the three occasions has its element, not only of inner experience, but of revelation from without: each is described as accompanied by a 'voice from heaven'. This awareness of correspondence between human event and spiritual environment was confined at the Baptism, to the two principal actors in the scene, the Lord and the Baptist, or possibly even to Jesus Himself; at the Transfiguration, it was extended to the disciples: on the third occasion, though the significance of the 'Voice' was clear only to Jesus, there was a confused awareness among the onlookers. To our Lord it was a declaration of the eventual glory and fruitfulness of His approaching Death, coming at a moment when He felt its approach with great clearness, shrank from it intensely, and yet realized that it was the fulfilment of His whole life and purpose, and that by it alone He could extend God's Kingdom to the world. Thus, in these days immediately before His Death, we see Him looking far into the future and claiming a universal right to attract the whole world. 'I, if I be lifted up, will draw all men unto myself.'

If the claim of Jesus Christ that His Death was to have a universal and saving power can really be true, then indeed He does stand before the world as a Figure of universal significance. If it is also true that nothing else has as deep a power of salvation, then the Christian religion is at least potentially universal, though its potentiality may never be wholly actualized upon earth. The universal claim of Christianity, which is so amazing when regarded with detachment, is thus seen to rest principally, not upon its moral teaching, nor upon the conscious grasp and acceptance of formulated doctrine. It rests upon the Salvation of the world by Christ Jesus, and upon this salvation as at once necessary and complete.

This saving character of Christianity, for several reasons, has been both discredited and obscured; discredited by its association with 'revivalist' methods, new and old, and their dangerous emphasis on emotion, and obscured by the tacit identification of Christianity with activities of brotherly kindness. As for the first, there is undoubtedly an emotional and non-rational devotion to the Person of Jesus regarded as the whole term of Christian worship, which has been a Christian weakness and cause of antagonism in others, though devotion to Jesus in its deeper and truer form is the whole source of Christian strength, and could not antagonize where it is understood. Perhaps more difficult to meet is the growing assumption that Christianity is identical with charity and mercy, and that men can practise this mutual loving-kindness in their own strength, if they choose, and do not need Divine rescue and rehabilitation at all. But to finer and wiser minds the offence of the Cross lies deeper. They know the frailty and insecurity of man's good intentions, his persistent self-centredness, and the violent force of his desires and emotions, and they realize that the problems and dangers of human nature are incalculably great. They believe that in seeking to solve them, by every human means and in the light of every advance in knowledge, they are humbly co-operating with a higher Power. But to offer them, as a solution, a mythical soteriology, no more credible to their minds than the worship of Mithras, appears simply an anachronism, a deliberate attempt to live on in the mental childhood of the race. Christian believers are bound to regard this attitude of complete scepticism with respect and sympathy, the more so because it is often combined with admiration for the work and teaching of Jesus in the Gospels, and by a desire to imitate Him in His lifelong efforts to heal and remedy suffering. It can truly be said of many who are sincerely offended by what they regard as the mythical in Christianity:

> *They know not Christ as Saviour,*
> *But worship Him as King.*

A presentation of the Atonement in terms which intelligent and sceptical people would find rational and credible is a true work of evangelism still waiting to be done.

Yet even from this agnostic point of view, there are considerations which favour an hypothesis of Divine intervention, and of its operation, not simply through the gradual use and training of human agents, but through decisive acts. The sense of sin as pollution and separation from God which characterizes religious experience everywhere, the inadequacy of human beings to redirect their own wills, and the high conception of God's own Nature which religion has formed, are great facts of our mental or actual history which make such a possibility at any rate not irrational. It must be placed among the conceivable interpretations of the mystery of life, that there has been a breach in our fellowship with God, and that the Nature of God is such that He must seek, and therefore has sought, to remedy it.

The deep sense of sin as uncleanness and separation which seems inherent in religion is admittedly, at many stages, not a moral quality at all, but a sense of almost physical defilement. Yet in the higher forms of all religions this sense of uncleanness is utilized and developed, and given a deep moral content: it is no longer ceremonial pollution, but actual wrong-doing, which is felt to separate man from God, and sacrifice means, not merely ritual acts

60

and offerings, by which the Divine favour is procured, but a worshipful self-giving to a Being whose Nature deserves it.

It might be expected that as this sense of the moral nature of sin became more delicate and acute, and the sense of God's goodness deepened, these enhanced perceptions would themselves be the remedy. Yet just as the highest conceptions formed of the Divine Nature left men dissatisfied and with a groping sense of incapacity, so the developing power of man to make moral distinctions even of the deepest and finest, has brought little apparent power to redirect his will.

'*Video meliora proboque, Deteriora sequor,*' remains, broadly speaking, Everyman's history, and the human misery for which mankind is responsible (whatever cosmic disorder may exist apart from him) is the sum total of these individual wrong preferences and aims. We are interlocked in the solidarity of a common humanity, so that what affects one affects all: and the result of this tragic interdependence can be seen as we look outwards and backwards over the whole course of time. The great symbolic pictures of the Book of Genesis place the disease of humanity rightly, in the will deflected by a lesser attraction from what is known to be good: and we begin to understand, as we see the motif reproduced in our own lives and in all history, something of what is meant by the Fall of Man.

To describe it as a 'Fall' lays the right emphasis upon the other, and positive, part of human history; it maintains with challenging force that the original and fundamental part of human nature is not the tendency to desire and choose wrongly, but the aspiration towards good. The doctrine of the Fall teaches, in fact, 'original' goodness rather than 'original' sin. Wrong desires, wrong acts, wrong choices, account for much of the human scene as we know it; yet the conserving and creating power in our history is the desire, varying and flickering and yet persistent, for beauty, order and goodness. Deeply as we are involved in one another's wrong-doing, the thoughts, motives and acts, which lead each of us, in different ways and degrees, towards the ordering and bettering of our life, make a still closer interdependence of goodness without which society could not exist at all. A society where there is perfect community and interdependence of wholly good activities is something which we can conceive, and this beauty and harmony is the ideal of human nature, though we remain unable to create it for ourselves. 'For the good which I would I do not: but the evil which I would not, that I do.'

For the cure of so diseased a world there are, conceivably, two alternatives, its dissolution or its healing, and in theory either of these lies within the power of God. But for the Nature which informs the Divine Power, and which is itself that Power, only the healing choice is really possible; though our categories of love and power may be so different from His as to explain much in life which seems mysteriously inequitable, it is the negation of thinking to suppose that the Divine Goodness can be less good, in terms of human understanding, than the imperfect goodness of men. In relation to an hypothesis of God's Existence, the redemption of man is a necessity rather than a probability: His Nature must necessarily include all the goodness found in His creatures, and His being must conform to the initial law of entity, that of being what it is: 'He cannot deny Himself.'[1]

This general conformity, in spite of all difference, between the Divine and human nature, might almost be

[1] 2 Timothy ii, 13.

called a favourite line of thought in the New Testament. Our Lord defines it for us with particular clearness in three parables, two of property and one of love, which hold a bright candle to the world of the unseen, and illustrate God's Nature, necessarily expressed to us in human terms, by the human instincts of ownership and paternity. The world which is shown to us by the light of the three parables, of the lost sheep, the lost coin, and the lost child, is one of vast extent and spaciousness: it is a world where the Will of God is joyfully fulfilled by the great majority of His creatures, who live in a close and intimate relationship with God and share His feelings and interests; and where the loss or perversion of even a small part of this creation is regarded as the loss of something infinitely precious. The Divine response is not resignation to this little loss, but diligent unwearying action to retrieve it: the Divine love appears to be undiminished, and even heightened, by the need and depravity of His creature, as a father's love is called out in greater intensity by the fault of a child. The action of God towards humanity will necessarily far surpass our comprehension; but it may be expected to have some recognizable correspondence with the observed characteristics of our world, and these parables suggest to us, by clear firm analogies, the main lines of this correspondence. No one who has reflected much on human nature can wholly exclude the possibility that the Being who is the source of our being has, at some time and in some way, poured out Himself for us in such an activity of search and sacrifice as men exhibit, where possession or natural affection is concerned. The strength and intensity of human instincts, and the power, resource and energy with which they are defended, should give us some faint idea of the strength and effectiveness of such a Divine intervention in human affairs, and should prepare us for results which will shake and change the whole process of history.

It can be argued that this is too anthropomorphic a view, that it goes beyond any conceivable human knowledge of God's Nature and endows Him with human personality; but this is not really true. It is true indeed that those who come into union with God in prayer may gradually come to know Him as Person and to find that His Nature is Love: but prayer is not a purely logical experience, and its mighty and massive evidence is not quite relevant here. All that need be maintained, to give at least probability to an act of Redemption, is that the Being who is the source and ground of a world that includes human personality must somehow include in His Nature all the energies of love and power which express themselves humanly in men and women, just as He must somehow include in Himself all the grace and beauty that expresses itself in the line and form of a tree.

Of the historical form which such redeeming action would take men could have no preconception, unless it were given through the glints and lights of an intuition deepening into prophecy. But it is certain that any true salvation of human nature must have two characteristics. It must reach down into the depths of the individual soul and empower the will to choose rightly: but it must achieve this end through a free and co-operative activity and without the smallest use of compulsion. This limiting condition will have one important result. Not only in the initial crisis of its advent, but at every stage of its long task of re-creation, the saving action of God can only succeed by appearing to fail; for if it is to be a true salvation, free and unconstraining and yet completely penetrative, its whole life and process must be an infinite patience which waits upon the growth of each individual soul, and upon a response which will often be indefinitely delayed. The real powers of rehabilitation which have been imparted or made accessible will often remain unrecognized or undeveloped: and if, as seems inevitable, human beings must help to extend knowledge and understanding of the Divine action to others, the inadequate response of these human instruments themselves will be a further hindrance to the outflowing grace of God. It might almost be said, though it is a humbling thought, that one of the 'characteristical marks' of a Divine redemption which is to extend to the whole world will be frustration over long periods of time, and rarity of any immediate or conspicuous success.

Christian theology recognizes, in the life and work of Jesus, such a saving and re-creating act of God, operating towards the world as a whole, and not merely towards one part or time: it is a central curative act which looks both backwards and forwards in its results, and reorganizes the whole time-process into the unity of God. This conviction was more than a gradual development brought about by the extension of Christianity: though the admission of Gentile converts caused it to be more fully realized and formulated, it was implicit from the beginning. Explicit statements like those of St. Paul, 'God was in Christ, reconciling the world to Himself', or of St. John, 'We have seen, and bear witness, that the Father sent the Son to be the Saviour of the world', elucidate and define, but do not alter, the meaning of the whole record. The Apostles regarded the Old and New Testament as essentially one, and their own apostolate as a fulfilment of Israel's mission to the whole world, and it is evident that they drew both these convictions from our Lord Himself. The Church was from the very beginning, much more than a society of the faithful, occupied with its own spiritual growth and welfare; it was a converting society facing outwards as well as inwards: and the Apostles were the ambassadors of a Divine reconciliation, which was the climax of the whole past history of Israel. But the method by which this reconciliation was to reinstate the individual was not ultimately the method of exterior action manifesting the Divine power: it was the re-creating of the individual life from within through his free acceptance of the gift of the Holy Spirit, which would redirect his whole self into the attitude of an ever-deepening response. Thus they regarded themselves as bringing to the world something concrete and historical, rooted in the past and subject to the canons of evidence, yet limitlessly individualized and capable of application to every person or situation of the future. Here, as it seems, there is a hint of conformity with those characteristics, noticed in a former chapter, of what is universal in our other experience. If only for this reason, it will be worth while to look closely at this purported reconciliation, which Christian theology calls the Atonement, and to look at it in two ways: from without, to see where it stands in history; and from within, to consider whether it really does show those necessary marks of a true redemption—the restoration and re-orientation of the individual soul, with searching completeness but without the least trace of compulsion. It is with these thoughts in our minds that we approach to a closer study of the Christian doctrine, at first so amazing in its incredibility, that 'the Father sent the Son to be the Saviour of the world'.[1]

[1] I John, iv, 14.

Chapter Five

THE JUDAIC PREPARATION

The Christian believer regards the Old Testament, naturally and inevitably, as a preparation for the New, though, like the other means of preparation, this does not rob it of its own special and independent value: and this double character in it causes him no difficulty. He has in his hands as it were, an Ariadne thread, and by this can feel his way backwards from the end to the beginning. The case is very different, if he places himself for a moment at the outside point of view, from which his faith and hope seem a tissue of assumptions. The Bible, and the Old Testament in particular, is less familiar than it was, or, even if known and valued, is treasured for literary greatness or for its general contribution to the upward movement of human history: the finest appreciation can here co-exist with entire disregard of its significance as a preparation for Christ. The Messianic hope of the Jews, the Davidic Kingship, the figure of the Suffering Servant in Isaiah, the fulfilment of both the Law and the Prophets in the Life, Death, and Resurrection of Jesus, are conceptions of which it is even too much to say that most people disbelieve them. They belong to an alien world and are regarded, where they are remembered at all outside the Christian Church, as remote and faded archaisms. Whatever historical significance they had, as shaping the early contours of Christianity, now belongs, for the great majority, wholly to the past, and the ablest expositions of the subject can be studied without any effect upon belief. The carefully presented evidence has the effect of a tapestry or painting, which can be better appreciated as the details are better seen: the grandeur and consistency with which the Old Testament converges upon the One Figure of Jesus is admired from outside the picture, as the Figure of Adam is admired in the Sistine roof. When the reared comes to consider the importance of what he has grasped and admired so fully, and to give it its place in history, he does indeed allow it significance, but only as a great and classic example of an abiding human tendency, the tendency to interpretation after the event.

Yet it is right that this whole picture, as the Christian sees it, should be placed clearly within the general view: and there may be some eye, among the spectators, to which its meaning will come unexpectedly home. At the least, it is not irrational that the redeeming love of God, as well as diffusing itself generally through the whole of mankind, should concentrate upon one place and time especially, and upon the training of one people to be the focus of its intensest rays. It is difficult to see how, in a world which has space and time as the form of its consciousness, and variety and inequality of gift as the form of its society, God's love could be wholly mediated to mankind in any other way. It is not irrational and may even be probable, and in the sphere of speculative truth no more than this ever can be said: here, even more than in the world of action 'probability is the very guide of life'.[1] But it must be re-emphasized here, and can hardly be too much emphasized, that the religious consciousness does not depend for its existence on the speculative processes, or look to them for final confirmation. It provides them with a vast field for their activity, but it does this by the

[1] Butler, *Analogy*, Introduction.

very fact that it exists in its own right. The heart's relationship with God, like any other human relationship, is a complex reality in which thought, emotion and will are all blended, and—just as in all valuable relationship—it is a life's work to give each element in it true proportion and to harmonize them in one whole: it is a life's work, and a work in which the whole personality is engaged and by means of which it grows. Again, just as all fruitful human relationships deepen the understanding of life and open up fresh fields of view, so the deepening growth of the heart's relationship with God means that the whole of life is seen with a wider expansion and illumination of the intellect: the mind looks, as it were, from a new viewpoint and the significant objects of the past stand out with a new proportion and clearness. The new vision which the first Christians obtained of history and which they expressed for us in the New Testament writings was exactly of this kind: it was a re-interpretation of their own previous knowledge in the light of their relationship with Jesus Christ, and anyone who desires to study the Christian re-interpretation of history must first study that relationship.

Yet even taken by itself and apart from any special interpretation, the religious history and development of the Jewish people provides indications, not only of the recognizable action of God in history, but of its redemptive quality and purpose It could be sketched in brief outline somewhat as follows: that God, who has at no time been lacking to any people, revealed certain indispensable truths of His Nature in unique measure to one people, who may therefore be called a people of unique religious genius: that these truths found expression in the Mosaic Law, in the ritual of the tabernacle and the temple, and in the teaching of the prophets: that Israel developed a unique sense of vocation, including—at the highest level of the prophetic teaching—a sense of being called to accomplish a great saving work for mankind as a whole: that this sense of vocation and future became associated with the hope of a revived Kingship in David's line, and of a Messiah through whom, supernaturally commissioned and endowed, God's purpose for Israel was to be accomplished. This developing sense of Divine vocation was accompanied, as one might expect, by markedly deepening apprehensions of the Divine character. The characteristic features of Israelite belief in God—the rejection of idolatry, the belief in His Unity and Personality and of His covenant-relationship with His people—are not indeed absolutely unique and it would be surprising if they were: what is unique is the strength, intensity and perseverance with which they are held; and this tenacious grasp of the commanding identity of God is combined with a broad, flexible, and ever-increasing consciousness of His complete control over history and His moral and spiritual requirements.

This intensity, precision, and range of thoughts are the notes of an incomparable literature. Even if the Wisdom books are excluded from consideration, as more eclectic in their origin, there is no real parallel, outside Palestine, to the total effect of the Book of Deuteronomy, the Prophets, and the Psalms: while at either extreme of these, in atmosphere and range, are the Book of Job, where God and man are brought into the deepest personal relationship, and the older part of the Book of Proverbs with a delicate and practical insight into human nature. The great glories of the Old Testament, the most sublime and famous passages of Isaiah, Job, or the Book of Psalms, are not isolated works of individual religious genius, they are rooted in a wide and deep context of historical development and reality, and it is this which gives such incisiveness to their grandeur, and strength to their great beauty.

THE JUDAIC PREPARATION

These authoritative convictions as to the Divine character and action, combined with a deepening sense of the demands involved, expressed themselves primarily in the prophets' sense of direct vocation, and in their deeper interpretation of worship and sacrifice. Their teaching is national rather than personal in its tone, and they set the ideal of social righteousness before their people, not as a humanitarian duty, but as a direct command from God of which they are urgently conscious. They are at war, not only with idolatry, but with conventional religion, centred in observance and detached from conduct, and they are intensely aware that such a religion is a national sin which will bring God's punishment. God is Lord of all history and ruler of all nations, and other nations than Israel will be His instrument of judgment. Formal sacrifices, without righteous and merciful conduct, are displeasing to God, in proportion as His mercies and teaching have been clear throughout Israel's history. Thus the prophets' main preoccupation, both before and after the Exile, is with their own country and with the crucial importance, for Israel itself, of Israel's response to God. Yet this same Israel is to be the centre and rallying point of other nations and their Teacher in the ways of God; and there are a number of passages, especially in the later portions of Isaiah—the passages which describe the Suffering Servant —which suggest a deeper conception of Israel's rôle, as suffering redemptively on behalf of the peoples who have received a less full revelation. The thought remained undeveloped, and in the centuries following the Return from Exile, religious consciousness was occupied interiorly, with the perfect keeping of the Law and with the quiet development of such an outlook as is seen, at its highest, in the 119th Psalm. Though this emphasis on observance of the Law led finally to a pernicious formalism, its true spirit, as it appears in this Psalm, and in much of the Book of Deuteronomy, was very different: it enshrined for many generations priceless truths of God's Unity and Personality and His claim on men, and provided an environment in which a deep interior spirituality could live and grow.

To this extent, in the years between the return from exile and the birth of Jesus Christ, the hope of Israel was turned inward upon itself. Yet it was in the innermost circle of this deep personal devotion that the national hope of a Messiah was most cherished, and had the widest range: it was to be the work of the Anointed King not only to redeem and restore Israel, but to lift up the light of a truer knowledge of God for all the peoples of the earth.

But the Law and the Prophets do not provide our only indications of a Divine utterance and purpose through Israel. It was in the primitive ideas of worship, propitiation, and sacrifice that we seemed to come closest to a real consciousness of the supernatural: if so, the redemptive self-disclosure of God will be bound to strike deeply into these fundamental conceptions and to utilize them, like everything else that is fundamental to human nature, permanently in the service of God and man. We are apt to put the Temple worship on one side as a primitive survival of animal sacrifice, or as valuable only for the moral and spiritual lessons drawn from it by the prophets. It is true that it was destined to be superseded and that it was the inspiration of great prophetic imagery and thought; but its ultimate value, like that of all worship, is to be found in itself. The sense of Power and Being external to the worshipper; the sense of uncleanness and separation, the need at once to propitiate and to be in close communion with the God—all these dim and potent instincts, which seem to be inherent in the religious consciousness, are found in the religion of Israel operating at their highest power. The sixth chapter of Isaiah, the opening chapters of Ezekiel with their imagery based on the temple worship, and the sixteenth chapter of Leviticus describing the ritual of the Day of Atonement, are perhaps the best single illustrations of this. In the last of these, the reality of sin and of the breach with God which it has caused are expressed with the gravity and intensity of a great cere-monial: the ritual is not a formality, but is the language in which the Jew could least inadequately communicate his national and personal consciousness. Here in the very heart of Israel's worship, we find the emphasis thus laid on the separating effects of sin and the need for reconciliation; and the solemn ritual which enshrines these ideas brings man once more into a close association with God, in a relationship of forgiven-ness.

The authors of the New Testament writings saw the ful-filment, in the Person of Jesus, both of the Messianic hope in all its forms, and of the inner realities of their worship. They identified Him with the Sufferer of Isaiah as well as with the Ruler and Deliverer who was to initiate a new age, and they recognized, in His Self-Offering on the Cross, at once the annulment of the Temple sacrifices, and the Divine fullness of their meaning. This identification is the unify-ing principle of all the New Testament writings, widely different in authorship and character as they are; and there seems no doubt that it goes still farther back and was an integral part of the teaching of Jesus Himself to the inner circle of His disciples. If so, the unity of New Testament thought and teaching has a simple and sufficing cause; and we are brought back to the conclusion that the student of Christianity, if he is to understand it historically, must fix his attention upon Jesus Christ, and must try, in all reverence, to understand His mind and His influence upon others.

THE JUDAIC PREPARATION

Yet this brief glance at the religious history of Israel has had its value, by showing its place in a very remarkable series. We have seen cause to believe that it is in harmony with the Divine Nature to desire and seek the redemption of our human nature 'weakened and wounded' by sin. It is at least noteworthy that, in addition to the widespread intuitions of God's Being and Power found all over the world, and the high and beautiful conceptions of His Nature in many parts of it, a single people should possess a religious history of unparalleled depth and concentration and should make the fruits of it available to the whole world in so great a literature: it is perhaps especially noteworthy that in some of the most searchingly beautiful passages of this literature, whatever their exact contemporary meaning, the thought of redemptive and vicarious suffering should be present beyond any doubt. There seems some real ground for the hypothesis that this nation was chosen by God, as individuals are chosen, to receive these revelations of Himself and to impart them in some way to the rest of the world: and it is difficult to find another explanation which gives coherence and intelligibility to all the facts.

Chapter Six

THE ATONEMENT

It is against this rich and complex background that we must place the doctrine of the Atonement, in which Jesus Christ is in some sense the representative victim, self-offered for the sins of humanity, and His death is an effectual reconciliation between man and God. But though the background and setting of the doctrine is of such rich and deep historicity, the consideration of this, as of any dogma, raises the question implicit in all doctrinal theology, and a stumbling-block to many minds. The precise and guarded terminology of doctrine seems to represent a transference of the abstractive and generalizing tendency in human thought to the sphere of religion, where it is least appropriate. While the doctrine of the Atonement is linked, at one extreme, with the most primitive religious conceptions, it has been shaped by this generalizing process at the other. Between an origin in the deep recesses of inner consciousness, and a long subjection to the arid process of ratiocination, it seems almost too easy to account for the growth of doctrine. Truth and reality seem, in the analysis, almost to vanish away. For the believing Christian no answer to this question is necessary, because no such difficulty can be felt; but it is a real barrier to those who are genuinely seeking an honest intellectual basis for the nature of their faith. It is therefore worth considering whether—quite apart from the convictions which only long and consistent experience can give—there may not after all be

75

some indication that the method of analysis is not the last word; that a doctrine cannot be fully accounted for and its reality dissipated, by a resolution into its component parts.

Again, as in the consideration of universality, the knowledge which is common to human experience may suggest, if not a complete answer, at any rate a profitable opening for thought. It would seem that our sense-apprehensions and all our *a priori* knowledge, as of relation and number, never give us a knowledge of the nature of reality, but only of the form under which we apprehend it. There are certain things which we know with comprehension, with the sense, that is, of a whole and complete grasp. We comprehend the proof of a proposition, are completely satisfied with the conclusion and understand each step of it; but this kind of knowledge always seems to be achieved by the gradual processes of thought and reasoning. Further, all our comprehended knowledge, which is a knowledge of something limited, has underlying it the assumptions of our *a priori* knowledge, and would be impossible without it; and this *a priori* knowledge is clear indeed and unmistakable, yet is the expression of an inexplicably mysterious and perhaps limitless unknown.

These considerations are applicable to the whole human apprehension of God, as the form of an incomprehensible Reality by means of which we assemble orderly systems of thought and conduct; and they can be applied with especial propriety to Christian thought. Fundamental to their thought, for Christian believers, are certain unshakable convictions: of the Living Presence and Power of their Lord; of the effectiveness and completeness of His self-offering for the world; of their own indefeasible right to unite with it the little offering of their own lives, and so give these lives a share in the value and efficacy of His. Their life is a continuing and deepening apprehension of

His Personality, living and effective in His Church: their knowledge of Him is the form of their experience of God, and their whole power depends on these fundamental apprehensions of God in Christ, by which they 'live and move and have their being'. Those who seek to evaluate religious experience have paid great attention to its individual diversities, but perhaps not quite enough to the existence of these solid and, in essentials, uniform convictions about the Person of Jesus. These convictions are deep, immovable, and lasting: yet they seem independent, in the majority of cases, of any direct consciousness of His Presence, or of any religious experience which gives emotional satisfaction. They are based on experience, it is true, and of a lasting and important kind, but not the experience of any personal revelation or even sensibility. It is, first, the whole experience of the whole body of Christian believers, from the call of the first disciples until now, and secondly, the practical and self-observable result, for each individual life, of their decision to accept the Lordship of Christ and to be one of His company of disciples. Formulated Christian doctrine is an attempt to put into as clear language as possible that sum total of Christian experience about the living and continuing work of Christ. Rather than a rationalized abstraction of primitive religious ideas, it is of the nature of a general definition drawn from a vast body of instances, and must be studied with the respect due to such definitions, which are, each in its own sphere, among the most constructive achievements of human thought.

Every central Christian doctrine has, however—and this needs never to be forgotten—another, and a fundamental derivation: for it derives from the authority of Jesus Christ, either as expressed in His own teaching about His Person and Work or as conveyed to us through His Apostles and their near companions. Christian belief is grounded on this authority, and the Christian can no more doubt here than he can doubt, for the page which he is reading, the evidence of his eyes. But if he is led to consider the intellectual basis of this really existing and unquestionable faith, every Christian becomes, in the strict sense of the word, a sceptic. Untold confusion has been caused by the error that scepticism, as an attitude of mind, has some connection with religious doubt. For reasoning purposes, believer and unbeliever alike must adopt an attitude of strict inquiry: and a fully formed and adult faith is a growth from these two long processes; from trust in the authority of Jesus Christ and from observation of Christian experience, through which those elements of Christian truth which were first received as authoritative reassemble themselves, as it were, by an inductive process, from the experience of individuals. We are to seek, that is to say, in matters of doctrine, just that correspondence—massive, varied, and long-continued—between authority and experience which, as was suggested in an earlier chapter, even the authority of our senses requires.

It is in this twofold character, as indicated about Himself by the greatest Figure in history and as the lived experience of succeeding generations, that we can contemplate the Atonement. It has a twofold character, yet very different from the former duality, when it appeared to be compounded from primitive religious ideas and from the tendency to rationalize them. It does indeed satisfy and respond to the deepest intuitions of man's first religious consciousness, and to the fullest range of his intellect, but it is not rooted in either and has substantial existence of its own. We can fairly make the hypothesis that, in studying it, we are at close quarters with that remedial action of God upon humanity which our condition requires, and which we have seen it to be probable that God's Nature will give.

The whole life of Jesus Christ constitutes, *ex hypothesi*, this saving action by which the human race, and through it the whole creation, is bound once more closely to God in the right harmony and fellowship. The saving action culminates in the Death on the Cross, but the Death and the Life are one process, continuing onward into the Life of the Resurrection: and the isolation of our Lord's Death from this whole process can only lead to misconception. Throughout, He was engaged in a great cosmic war against the powers of evil, for the rescue of creation and for its reunion with God. He did, in fact, achieve this rescue and reunion, and though the means by which He did so are many-faceted in beauty and mystery, they can be expressed broadly and generally in two ways: first, that He offered to God on our behalf throughout His whole Life and Death a perfect, freely willed, entirely loving obedience, in compensation for the disobedience of sin; and secondly, that His Death, which was the crown and climax of this obedience, constitutes an effectual 'sacrifice, oblation and satisfaction, for the sins of the whole world'.

It is easy to understand that a stainless perfection of obedience, unbrokenly and faultlessly maintained throughout the whole of a human life, might, and indeed must, be an integral part of the work of restoration, and that such a life, once lived, could not only provide mankind with an endlessly fruitful example but could be a new organic start: the Love and Life of God, directed manward, would at last find a focus of perfect health, in which it could operate unhindered. It is at first a little difficult for us to see why the necessary culmination of this obedience was the Death on the Cross; nor can we expect ever to do otherwise than stand here in awe, in the face of a great

79

mystery. There is assuredly here no vengeance, no penalty exacted by God: it would be truer to say that here is the Divine Love operating in conditions of evil, and the Divine Humility submitting itself to the worst that evil can do, in order to triumph over it by sacrifice. Our whole human experience gives us an intuition of the appropriateness of this, and of the necessarily sacrificial character of even a true human love. But it is right that we should try to understand as far as possible with our minds the meaning of something so vital to the whole interpretation of life as is the Christian doctrine of the Atonement: the attempts of Christian theology from the beginning to give it intellectual expression have been right in their emphasis, even when tentative and ephemeral in their form.

Humanly speaking, our Lord's death was inevitable: for the whole tenor of His action, and the authority which He exercised, were such as to bring Him into acute conflict with a powerful Jewish Church. It is the more striking that from the very beginning the Apostles attached a further significance to His Death and Resurrection than that of a supreme injustice and a Divine vindication of innocence. The Death was an act of vicarious reparation for human sin; it was a substitution for the death of the human race as a whole, and it was an effective substitution in that it meant the possibility of a fresh beginning; and it was in accordance with the will of God. St. Paul expresses all this in dramatic language when he describes the Death on the Cross as an identification of Christ with human sin; but it is the mind of the Christian Church that he is expressing, and not a view of his own. 'Him who knew no sin, He made to be sin on our behalf that we might become the righteousness of God in Him.'[1]

There are thus two difficulties in the doctrine of the

[1] 2 Cor., v, 21.

Atonement, which need to be clearly distinguished: the difficulty of seeing how an act of Christ can in any circumstances be a substitution for ours, and the difficulty of understanding why, even if the possibility of substitution be accepted, the necessary form of it must be bodily suffering and death. A perfect life culminating peacefully in a holy and tranquil death, might seem to be the natural prelude to a Resurrection of the spirit-perfected Body of Christ and Its Ascension into the heavenly places, there to be the abiding centre of contact between Earth and the life of Heaven. Thus the Cross does not seem at first a necessary condition even of the Resurrection itself, and the necessity of Christ's suffering startles us now as it did the first disciples. We receive a shock of discordancy and horror, each time we begin to approach the Passion once more in our imagination. It appals us that He, the healer and physician to all kinds of human suffering, must Himself be subjected to the extremest suffering and to all forms of physical and mental anguish: and our hearts and minds protest against its necessity. 'Be it far from Thee, O Lord!' comes as naturally to our lips as to Peter's, when we begin to contemplate the possibility of the Cross.

The first of these difficulties, though it looks so formidable, is in reality much the slighter of the two. Real and effective substitution is an integral part of human life, and developed society would be impossible without it. In every part of our life we are dependent on actions performed not only for our advantage, but in our stead: and such actions are better and more effectively performed than if we ourselves had been the doers. When a pair of shoes is made for us, or our food prepared for us, we are substituting another's energy for our own: and where, as happens in an organized society, we can choose skilled workers, the result is more adequate to its end than our own less skilled activity. Even in mental work, when we use the mind of another, as in some great classic of philosophy, to guide us through a necessary train of thought, we are substituting that mental energy for our own, to lead us into understanding. Even in aesthetic appreciation, we take the enlarged and refined experience of some great critic and apply it to the work we are contemplating, and the more enlightened judgment which we can ourselves bring to works of art later was only made possible by our use, in the first instance, of another's mind. The individual is not an isolated unit, and his growth in individuality is in fact wholly dependent on his substitution, in a variety of ways and in an ascending series, of the activity of others for his own. Substitution can be harmful, it is true, and can arrest growth: but it is harmful only when the activity could have been as adequately performed by the individual as by the substitute to whom he resigns it. In such case the surrender of his personal activity will hinder his true development, but in all other cases it will promote it.

We need not fear, therefore, to use the word substitution of the work of Jesus Christ, as if it meant some shifting of our personal responsibility. He was able to perform more adequately than any one of us that which is the highest activity of a human being and involves the whole of human nature—the worshipful self-offering of the whole self to the Highest; and the essential preliminary to our own progress must be the whole-hearted acceptance and utilization of His substituted power. What the great thinker does for us in the region of thought, with a power and perfection far beyond our capacity, what the artist does for us in the region of beauty, and every skilled workman for us in the sphere of his own skill, Jesus Christ does for us in the region of personality. Each of these other substitutions, when we utilize them fully, carries us to a higher level in that particular sphere, but each is concerned only with a part of life. In living for us a whole human life throughout at the highest level possible, our Lord—for so here we can first most truly name Him—provides us with a total environment of perfection: only in so far as we are completely surrendered to this environment can we reproduce its character in ourselves. The infinite perfection of our Lord was offered on our behalf as a substitution for our imperfection, but because of this very fact, and not in spite of it, it is an wholly indispensable means.

Much deeper and more difficult is the second question, the necessity of Christ's suffering as an integral part of the sacrificial offering. Yet, deeply mysterious as this part of His work must always be to us, it is not in conflict with the rest of our experience. It is a simple and tragic fact that good endeavour of any kind draws out the hostility of whatever is wrong in its environment. The more fully a life is devoted to good ends, the more evident is the clash of these incompatibles, and the result is, in one form or another, suffering. It is doubtful whether any great good can be wholly achieved except at the cost of much suffering and, in most cases, of death. It may be the cruelties of war and a soldier's death in battle: it may be unjust condemnation and execution, as in the case of Socrates and St. Joan: it may be sickness and death, because the self-expenditure demanded by the special task has worn out the body before its time: but in one or another of these ways, it would seem that any work of supreme value exacts a sacrificial dying from its leaders and pioneers. This is outstandingly true of those whose work, like that of Socrates, penetrates into human life and history with effects which prove to be lasting. The conflict of good and evil which culminates in the physical defeat of the indi-

THE ATONEMENT

vidual, but the victory of his purpose, is no less true because mysteriously true; and if our insight were less confused by our own faulty condition, the element of mystery would be less. As it is, we accept this pain-producing conflict as a law of our present existence, and it leads us to expect that the remedial work of God, for and in humanity, would result in such a clash of good and evil, of especial intensity and violence. Just such an atmosphere, of ultimate conflict underlying all the immediate causes of our Lord's trial and execution, permeates the Calvary narratives; and the rest of the New Testament is wholly concerned with the results and first episodes of His victory.

Our Lord's Passion was thus a necessary result of His own dedication to good; and it was essential to the completeness of His substitution. If He was to go before us in the work and way of perfection, that perfection must be exhibited in the crucial conflict of human life, the conflict between good and evil: only by living out our humanity perfectly through the resulting conditions of pain and death, could He provide the existing reality of an entire human perfection into which we can enter, and conquer in our turn by absorbing its character into our lives. At whatever point of view we stand to look at the Cross, we see that the Christ who suffered and died there, did so for our sake and in our stead. His death was what the Church has called it from the beginning, a saving death on our behalf; for as the crown and completion of victory over evil, it saved us from a death which, sooner or later, and in one way or another, our race must have died: it arrested —potentially for all—the downward trend of humanity. It was a death in our stead; for in conjunction with His whole life it achieved a victory of which we have shown ourselves incapable: and it was a perfect offering, for us and instead of us, of a perfectly loving obedience to the

84

loving Fatherhood of God. Yet the meaning of the sufferings of Christ is not exhausted when we have seen them as essential to His victory. Suffering is not only the result, and inevitable accompaniment, of the conflict between good and evil: it is not purely a waste-product as it were, generated in the clash of conflicting forces; or, even if something like this were its origin, it is capable of utilization which carries it far from its beginnings and gives it supreme value of its own. We see this very clearly in the use made of suffering by many who are called to endure it. Its evident fruits are the qualities of patience, strengthening and steadying the whole character and environment, and of enlightened sympathy with the suffering of others. Less evident, but not less real, is the deliberate offering up of both physical and mental suffering, as an intercession for others' needs. We cannot judge the exact result of such intercession, in the warp and woof of the whole; yet at the very least, it deepens the offerer's own power of loving and giving, and thus helps, if only at this one point, to loosen the compacted tangle of human selfishness: and both probability and all the available evidence suggest that it has wider results and some effects for others. We should expect to find this utilization of suffering carried, in our Lord's Life and Death, to its highest power: and this has in fact been the consistent teaching of His Church. Christ's sufferings were, it is true, the means of His perfection in the human qualities of patience, humility and tenderness, and the example for ours, but they were more than that. The whole of His Passion was taken and used by Him as reparatory suffering, freely willed and offered, and boundlessly penetrative in its effects. The most glorious part of His work in the Atonement is not the victory over evil, mighty and glorious as it was, but the utilization, for all time, of His suffering as the means of our purified and regenerate life. The Death on the Cross was an embodied intercession, with effects both catastrophic and gradual on the events and tendencies of the future. The first phase, as it were, of the work of our At-one-ment with God is necessarily negative and destructive, concerned with the release of our capacities from the prison-house of sin and death, but it leads on, for each individual and for humanity as a whole, to what is constructive and positive, concerned with light and freedom, and the building up of our redeemed nature into a new righteousness: and the Agent of this work, on the Cross and in Eternity, is the embodied sacrifice of our Lord.

Chapter Seven

THE MEANS OF REGENERATION

Concern and even preoccupation with material things
is a characteristic of primitive religion: supernatural power
is felt to be centred in external objects, both animate and
inanimate, and to affect man, for good or evil, through
these. Many of these primitive fears and tabus are long-
lived, and persist into the later stages of a religion, although with diminished force; but the most truly sincere
and religious minds reject them utterly, as wholly incon-
sistent with the loving Providence of God. The result is
a tendency to go to the opposite extreme, and to deny the
material any part whatever in our spiritual life. Religion,
it is maintained, must be spiritual or it must be nothing
at all, and spiritual power can only be mediated by spiritual
means. The most explicit form of this view among Christians is the Society of Friends; but it is not confined to
Quakers, and is probably the most definite element in the
vague, generalized religious sense which strangely co-
exists, in our own era, with clear-cut hostilities to religion.
Yet in spite of the true spirituality in this rejection of the
material, it has very deep dangers. It is one thing to cast
magic and superstition on the rubbish-heap where they
belong; it is perilous, in doing so, to repudiate the connection between spiritual and material, which is part of
life as we know it and must be representative, in some way,
of life as it really is. Just as the primitive ideas of sacrifice
had to be discarded and yet contained fundamental re-

ligious truth, so primitive superstitions, in all their elaborate and often hideous forms, held a priceless core of reality. They brought home the fact that man's whole life as he knows it here is sustained by the material, is lived in and through the material, and that every form of experience of which he is capable comes to him, in the first instance, by material means. Our mind is not the originator but the orderer of those intimations of reality which are communicated to us through our senses; and the mind itself functions through an exquisitely delicate material organization. It is inconceivable that the spiritual part of man should exist, as it were, in a void and have no interaction with the rest of his experience: and nothing suggests that this is really the case. Man comes to realize, it is true, that his most valuable possessions are not ultimately material, but it is through life in a material world, and through analogies drawn from it, that he arrives at this realization. Any attempt to thrust the spiritual and the material into separate channels is finally disastrous; the material re-asserts itself, in one way or another, and takes terrible revenges. The instinct is right which in most religions accepts this coinherence of spirit and matter as the invariable means by which the supernatural enters human life, and no religion which does not allow for this can be completely and thoroughly penetrative of the whole life and personality.

When we look back, with this thought in our minds, to Christianity, we realize that the acceptance and utilization of the material, as the means of spiritual truth and power, is a keynote, from the very beginning of our Lord's ministry and through the whole history of the Church: no error and misuse of this principle by the Church at any stage must blind us to its importance. It is wholly fundamental to Christianity and an essential part of its saving character. The whole material world in and by which we live has been defiled by sin and by the self-centred use of its gifts; this misusing has weakened human strength and capacity and has made the human scene one of pain and sorrow. The effects have not only been moral and physical: they have penetrated to the intellect and deeper still, to the innermost shrine of personality. Man's vision is narrowed and his apprehension of reality darkened, from the moment that he ceases to regard the material as in some sense an expression of the spiritual, and considers it as a thing in itself. Whether he then tries to discount and discard it as much as possible, or to treat it as the fundamental form of reality, is of less importance. Whichever he does, he has divided what should be one, and his thought is the expression of a radical incoherence. There seems ground for thinking that the real universe, which we apprehend through its varied aspects, is a unity and a whole; if so, we shall become aware of that unity and wholeness only in so far as we appreciate the organic character of our existence and the interdependence of our earthly and spiritual life. Flashes and hints of this realization come to all of us, particularly through our apprehensions of beauty in nature and art; but we all fail and come short of its fullness, and to the extent that we do so there is a rift in the integrity of the self. We are born, it would seen, with this lesion: it is beyond our power to remedy and we find it difficult to imagine life without it. But we realize that, in its absence, our sense experience would be, habitually and naturally, the gateway of insight into realities beyond it, and would be the means, with an equal simplicity and naturalness, by which the power and grace of the spiritual world could enter into our lives and build us up into the likeness of its ineffable beauty.

This failure to grasp the relation between parts of our

experience is a result that might readily follow from a mis-use of one of those parts. It is hardly too much to say that it would be bound to do so, and this disjointed and frag-mentary view of reality is part of the disorder that comes from human sin. This takes us a little further and helps us in forming some conception of the Divine power at work in the process of healing and restoration. We shall expect of this remedial action that it will be effective in two ways; that it will give man a fresh vision of the external world as a lesson-book of spiritual truth, and that it will operate through the human person and environment, making them the channels of spiritual grace and power. It is difficult to see how otherwise there could be a real At-one-ment, or how else the saving action could be really penetrative of human personality, reaching into the self in its fundamen-tal ground and reorganizing it without suppression or mutilation. It is the more impressive, when we return to the New Testament, to see how completely, and in both ways, the Life and Death of Jesus Christ fulfils this expec-tation. His whole teaching centres on the essential unity of the earthly and heavenly worlds, and He uses the one as an alphabet to explain the other. He accepts the great sym-bols of the Old Testament ritual and points to their fulfil-ment in Himself. Yet He does not only treat the material universe as a parable of the heavenly: He uses it as the instrument through which new power is conveyed. He uses touch, and even clay, in His healing. He takes a small portion of bread and uses it for the nourishment of thou-sands. He seems, moreover, to be preparing the minds of His disciples for a time when not only the body, but the spirit of man will be refreshed and strengthened by a new life, given through material signs. In clear yet mysterious utterances, He proclaims that His Death on the Cross will make this possible, and that His Father's purpose for mankind will be fulfilled through His own unqualified self-surrender. Listening to Him with attention, we begin to understand something of what is meant by the utilization of His suffering and the need for its finality. The mysterious frustration of human death had itself to be given positive value, if the new life from God was to penetrate every part of our human experience. 'The last enemy that is to be destroyed is Death', and the way of Death's destruction was not by evading it, but by using it as the very means of life in the spiritual world, as it was already used in the material. Thus, though the Resurrection of our Lord remains a *mysterium tremendum*, it is not meant to be entirely remote from our understanding; we can form some conception of its reason and meaning, even with our present capacities. It was into His Father's power, not the power of evil, that our Lord rendered His body and soul in the moment of His dying. He rendered them utterly, not for annihilation or consciousless absorption into the Divinity, but to become the living vessel of the Divine life and the means of its communication to all. With the Resurrection the deep severance in our experience began to be reconciled, and the Resurrection life, for each one of us, is the making of this reconciliation effective. Jesus, Risen, is the means of communion and the bond of unity, between the earthly and heavenly worlds.

Our Lord brought this home to the disciples, in the first place, by the material and physical character of the Resurrection appearances. We may lawfully think that He was careful to emphasize His continued bodily identity and the fact that there was no breach whatever between the material and spiritual. 'He did eat before them.' 'Reach hither thy hand and thrust it into my side.' 'Handle me and see. A spirit hath not flesh and bones as ye see Me have.' But this Body, which Death had entered and could not hold, was now the means by which the spirit and power of Christ could enter with a new directness into the hearts of His friends. The Ascension of this same Body into the heavenly places was to make that power accessible for all places and times.

The Ascension of our Lord into Heaven is an event which men could only conceive, or at least could only describe, in local and spatial terms, but it is none the less an event of transcendent reality and significance. The symbolic character of our spatial expressions—as indeed, in some degree, of our whole spatial experience—deepens rather than diminishes their value as an approach to truth. They are inadequate, not because they are too real and concrete, but because they are abstractions from just as much as we can apprehend of a reality which is rich and concrete beyond all our imagination. With this clear to our minds we are better able to consider the Ascension as immeasurably real and effective. If we could essay a description of it in, as it were, a kind of paraphrase, it would be something like this: that our Lord has lifted up humanity in His own Person to be in the Presence of God continually; and the Presence of God is a treasury of loving power, which is now made available, through the glorified Christ, to men. He is, in this sense, a Mediator, not as standing between us and God, but as the means, in His complete humanity and yet complete union with God, through which we can receive all the gifts of God as needed for our restoration. Intimate and effective contact is henceforward possible between God's power and man's need, between the greatness and transcendence of God and man's littleness and apparent insignificance.

Steady and solid thought on the Ascension is a wonderful corrective to many of our preconceptions and fears. The pathetic and terrifying contrast between the vast universe and our tiny planet loses, in the light of this, its power to distress and bewilder. We realize that power is not only independent of magnitude but different in its nature, and that Presence is something other than place as we know it: in so far as man lives in the Presence of God, he is no longer a stray atom of existence, but is living at the heart and centre of creation and looking out from it on to the universe. To forward the growth of this new life in every man and thus to centre him in eternity, is the work of the Risen and Ascended Jesus.

It will be expected that this extended ministry, operating at large throughout space and time, should bear the same marks as the earthly ministry of our Lord: should exhibit the same insistence on the personal and concrete and should operate through human agents and material signs and means. Even during His lifetime our Lord's use of human intervention was not confined to Himself. Not only the twelve Apostles, but the seventy or seventy-two of the first widespread mission were commanded to heal as well as preach, and their commission was for both mental and bodily healing. Then as now, they sometimes succeeded and sometimes failed: in so far as they succeeded, in that degree the extension of our Lord's power through other human agents had already begun, yet not without qualification. They were empowered for the healing of mind and body in the Holy Name of Jesus, but to bring His healing power into the fundamental ground of personality, there to remake the soul in its secret places, was beyond even the Apostles' commission, as far as we can tell, until after the Resurrection. Only the Son of Man, in His own Person, had 'power on earth to forgive sins'. The supreme achievement of His Passion was to make His whole re-creative power universally available, partly through His followers and especially those most deeply dedicated to His service, partly through that purification and reconsecration of the material universe which, in His lifetime, had already begun. The commonest things of everyday life, bread, water, oil and wine, were now to be the consecrated vehicles of the new life for which grace—χάρις, a word associated with all that is kind and lovely—seemed to the Christian community the appropriate name. The same principle is seen at work in the solemn laying-on of hands, practised by the Church from the beginning. The Risen Life in its extension to the world is simply the fuller expression of the life on earth. It reconsecrates our sense-experience, not simply by bringing it into a passive accord with the true life of the spirit but by using it as the means through which the eternal life is conveyed.

It is possible that too little thought has been given, during the last few centuries, to the metaphysical implications of this principle, which—amongst very much else that it does—brings the phenomenal and noumenal parts of our experience into an harmonious relationship. Yet though worthy of the deepest care and attention by those called to this special kind of thought, it is not the central aspect of regeneration. Each of us is aware that his senses and his intellect do not make up his whole experience and indeed do not even finally condition it. The control which he can obtain over his environment depends on something deeper than either, which determines his motives and directs his actions often without his being aware. Psychology has charted this unknown region, and the knowledge thus gained—even though as imperfect and liable to correction as the maps of the early geographers—is a help and safeguard. But it leaves the real dilemma unsolved. The ground of personality cannot be finally reached and influenced by any power which is like itself and therefore ultimately no stronger, yet until it is reached there can be no permanent modifications. Disciplined senses and an ordered intelligence can build a surface personality, strong enough to bear any but the severest shocks; but so long as the deepest fund of being is not completely penetrated by a power greater than itself, the personality is never wholly stabilized and its unity secure. The regeneration of humanity, to be real and effective, must be regeneration at the very root.

There is one power, according to the New Testament, and one only, which can thus penetrate into the depths of the soul and then build it up into its new life, as part of a redeemed community and yet a living and fruitful identity in itself. This power is the Holy Spirit of God, operating freely in our whole nature through our union with the Manhood of Jesus as He lives and reigns in Heaven. This limitless power of God necessarily extends throughout the created universe, but with infinite tenderness and humility comes close to man through his everyday needs and surroundings, by the spiritual use and penetration of the commonest things. Entry into the new life in Christ is through the sacrament of Baptism where the element of water is the vehicle of Divine grace, and the Christian's life is nourished and developed thenceforward by similar means. The supreme instance of this is the Holy Communion, but an understanding of this supreme gift is deepened when we see it as part of a whole. The Lord still ministers to His people, in their various needs, just as He fed, taught, healed, blessed and forgave the multitudes of Galilee, who were lost and shepherdless without Him. There is the same variety and flexibility, the same adaptation of means to ends, in His service to us now through His Church. Each of the sacraments serves a different requirement of our nature and state. In Confirmation and

Penance, in Holy Anointing for our help in sickness and dying, in Holy Orders and Matrimony for those called to them, we are in a continued and varied contact with the life of God, a contact which covers the whole range of experience. These sacraments are no less divine and spiritual because they are less general in their purpose and effect than the fundamental sacraments of Baptism and Holy Communion. In all alike, the living Christ is at work, ministering His Father's love to the world, through the lips and hands of His priests and through the simple and precious treasures of His creation: thus by a series of processes He entwines the life of Heaven intimately with that of earth. The Holy Spirit indwells the matter of each sacrament as profoundly as He indwells the human nature to which His gifts are conveyed, and this twofold indwelling is the restoration of wholeness to experience. The human spirit and its material environment are realized as a unity through the Divine Presence in both.

There is nothing magical in this way of regeneration and to realize this we need only bring our minds back constantly to the simple thought of God. He is what He is, and we have seen that He must contain in Himself at least all the highest that we can possibly imagine. He cannot therefore enforce us or work upon us mechanically without our co-operation. Though this co-operation and response of our wills may not always be fully conscious—and we should expect this where such deep realities are concerned—it must be there. On earth our Lord could not heal without the response of faith: He needs the same response now to the healing which He gives us from Heaven, and it is a part of our nature that we are capable of this response. It may sometimes be given at first vicariously, through the faith of others, but this is natural to the unity of the human family and to our still closer unity in the family of Christ. But in the long run, the individual response of the soul to God is indispensable to the fruit of any Sacrament. Deep calleth unto deep, spirit to spirit, although the means, during our life on earth, will be in accordance with our earthly conditions.

Nothing could be more remote than this from the tyranny of magic, and we need not even draw any hard-and-fast line between our sacramental life and the rest of our experience. In the whole of our present existence the action of God reaches us through external and visible signs, through Nature and Art, through the earth's gifts to us, through the presence and the writing of others. The sacraments do not contravene this principle and might be called its extreme instance, but they apply it in a different sphere. We saw that the difference between the religious consciousness itself and the rest of our capacities was a difference of subject-matter rather than the operation of different laws: so it is with the sacramental principle. The laws are the same, but they operate in a region farther away from consciousness, and are at once deeper, and more far-reaching, in their results. It is often and truly said that the action of God is not confined to the Sacraments. Yet we must not forget, in saying it, that the Sacraments themselves do not limit, but extend, His action in humanity. Far from being restricted and specialized in the sacramental gifts, the Divine Love secures in and through them its widest and freest scope. The realization of this gives us a clearer insight into the truly universal character of Christianity. The Love of God flows into and penetrates our lives in countless ways, but nowhere so deeply and directly as through Jesus Christ. The Sacraments are the ordinary and principal means of our contact with His redeeming love in Christ and with that saving activity which we have seen to be so utterly necessary: it would be strange indeed if this contact were to be confined to the few. It is true that the Sacraments are not and perhaps never will be universally received: the conscious acceptance of Jesus Christ by the whole world must wait for His Second Coming and all the unveiling of eternal truths which that implies. But the sacramental life of the Church has an outward as well as an inward movement: though the Sacraments are not received universally they are universal in their effects. Their results flow out far beyond those who immediately receive them, for each faithful recipient is himself a fresh focus of the redeeming love of God and has some rays of the Divine radiance reflected outwards from himself. The bold wording of the Embertide Collect 'Almighty God, our heavenly Father, who hast purchased to thyself an universal church by the precious blood of thy dear Son' is thus truer than would appear at first sight. Christianity is universal not only by its essential character and ultimate aim, but in its effect upon the world as a whole.

Chapter Eight

CHILDREN OF GRACE

We are now in a better position to see how far Christianity corresponds with that ideal picture of a universal religion which we sketched out earlier; and the correspondence is remarkable in many ways. It gives the fullest satisfaction to the intellect, for it is at once very simple and very profound, yet it is not primarily intellectual. It touches every part of life and its help is available in the simplest forms for all who are willing to receive it; it uses the whole of human personality without suppression and it leaves the will entirely unforced and free. When every possible criticism has been applied to its sources, it remains substantially historical in its origins and outlook, and is thus firmly attached and related to concrete life and to the history of the world. But the final test of any authenticity is its correspondence, not with thought or ideal, but with experience. Christianity is not exempt from the plain judgment of fact and must show a recognizable conformity with actual experience, over long periods of time. The effects which it claims to have upon believers and the world around them must be exhibited in concrete reality if they are to be credible at all. The mere multitude of those who believe is not a proof: purely subjective experience can be shared on a wide scale by a kind of contagion or by the desire to remain mentally sheltered and immature. The 'means of grace' must be plainly productive of holiness, and the faith of Christians will in the long run be judged, like everything else, by its results.

> *But Cristes lore, and his apostles twelve,*
> *He taught, but first he folwed it himselve,*

might well be the ironical answer of the world to the Church. 'I admit the harmony and beauty in the picture which you present to me, but I marvel at your *naïveté* in presenting it. I admit that no power except the power of God could penetrate your life or mine and rebuild it fundamentally, and that only a Divine solution for the ills of humanity could be effective. It is not the Empty Tomb that affrights me, or the Divine action in and through the material universe: it is the truly appalling contrast between your theory and practice. You offer me a solution for all my needs and questions, and a healing of the canker which I know to be at my heart. It would be a satisfying solution if it corresponded with the facts, but as it is I must reject it. I am tempted at times to take it seriously and I stretch out my hands towards it in longing, but each time that I do so, the reality checks me. I recoil from the beautiful form as if it were a spectre, when I see what you are.'

There can be very few believing Christians to whom the truth of this severe indictment has not pierced right home at some time in their lives. Either by a fresh realization of too low a level in their everyday life, or else through some revealing crisis, they have become sharply and vividly conscious of their failure. They are pledged by their profession to one aspiration above all—that their own lives may show the image of Jesus: but it is an ugly and self-darkened picture that they have given to those about them. What is true of the individual is true again and again of the Church in its collective life. If the Christ is once more despised and rejected it is partly His followers' fault, and the attitude of the Church to the world by which it is judged must be primarily penitence.

Yet the picture of failure, true and sad as it is, is not the whole landscape which a very sincere and careful study of the Church's history, even from the outside, seems to reveal. Such a study, faithfully and impartially carried out over a wide field, makes it less easy to deny the presence of a new quality, the stirring of a new spirit in men since the coming of Christ. We ought not to be too much dismayed at the faint or intermittent appearance of its working when we contemplate the whole mass of sinfulness which it must permeate and dissolve. The restoration of man to his supernatural status is truly the work of the Atonement, but it is a free gift to each of us which we can neglect or can use. Where it is accepted and used most fully we shall expect that its manifestations in every part of life will be of special delicacy and beauty, and in spite of much failure the total of evidence does appear to bear this out. The new universe growing up very gradually and secretly in the midst of the old is even lovelier than the first creation because of its intimate union with the Incarnate Lord.

> 'Tis not all we owe to Jesus,
>   It is something more than all,
> Greater good because of evil,
>   Larger mercy through the Fall.

When we turn back to the New Testament we find that this is the predominant note. The sense of new life, of organic union with Jesus Christ, the reality of the joyful gift given in Baptism, pervade it from beginning to end. ʽΕἴ τις ἐν Χριστῷ, καινὴ κτίσις · τὰ ἀρχαῖα παρῆλθεν · ἰδοὺ γέγονεν καινά.'[1] Here, as elsewhere, St. Paul's great gift of ex-

[1] 2 Cor., v, 17.

pression has given memorable form to the new awareness and in doing so has deepened it for his readers. But the whole tenor of the New Testament shows that it belonged to the common stock of Christian experience and teaching from the first. It was closely associated with Baptism, the fundamental Christian initiation, at once the death of the old life and the beginning of the new. The death was much more than the putting away of sinful desires and habits. It was an identification of the self with the death and burial of Jesus. The new life was not simply a higher form of existence for the individual. It was a communion in the Lord's Resurrection. St. Paul has again given classic expression to the teaching: 'We were buried with Him through Baptism into death: that as Christ was raised from the dead through the glory of the Father, we also might walk in newness of life.'[1] The likeness in wording, close at times and perhaps deliberate, between the 'Life and death' of Christian baptism and those of the pagan 'mysteries' must not blind us to the essential difference. Union with God in Christ Jesus was not union with a mythical Saviour-God, a type or emanation of the Supreme, but with a living Person. The Life, Death, and Resurrection of Jesus were not myth but seriously attested fact: the whole structure of Christianity in its life and teaching rested, and rests, upon these as foundations. Yet here again the spiritual experience of paganism had contained a deep core of reality. The craving of man for a new and different quality of life, to be gained by an act or process of dying, is an important part of the religious consciousness. The mystery religions had expressed it for centuries and in spite of gross and nonmoral elements had led many to a higher view of life. At their best they had helped to deepen and spiritualize

[1] Romans, vi, 4.

philosophy, even though in their worse forms they had degraded it into magic. When St. Paul wrote that life could only be gained through a death, he was saying what Jesus Christ had said clearly before him, but also what was natural and understandable for his Gentile hearers—more so in some ways than for ourselves. The whole conception of regeneration has become dim to our minds and grace is a word which has almost lost its meaning. The Divine Image imprinted in us and the Divine gifts at our creation, have ceased to be part of our ordinary stock of thought; almost unconsciously, we tend to regard man as a highly organized and developed animal. Theories of evolution, and discoveries which show the great antiquity of human life on this planet, have helped to make this outlook. They are fascinating and important in their own sphere of truth and they bring their own rich gift into the spiritual kingdom, but they are not relevant here. They are concerned with a different type of truth, with the wonderful structural origin and growth of man, not with his spiritual endowment and history. But there are other causes which have complicated and obscured our view, and these, just because they are more relevant, are more difficult to disperse. The beautiful term Grace has become so much associated with theological controversy that it has lost its reality for many truly religious minds. They dispense with it as belonging to a world of fine-drawn theological distinctions which seem to place a barrier between the seeking soul and God. In doing this they perhaps forget that wherever controversy, in theology as elsewhere, is intense and persistent, it is because of some vital importance in the subject-matter. But not everyone is called to the theologian's special task, part of which is the intensest application of human reason to the truths of faith. For the entrance of Grace into nature, the new life into the old, there is no need to look beyond the New Testament. It is there in the Gospels, as the seed in the soil, the leaven in the loaf, the hidden treasure, the all-precious pearl: it fills the whole thought and consciousness of the early Church. They were alive with a new life through the Spirit of Jesus and in proportion as they responded to it the former things were passed away and all things had become new.

Neglect to use the grace that is given and to let the Spirit of Jesus be the motive force in their lives is probably the chief cause of Christian failure, rather than great deliberate sin. The impression which many Christians make upon their environment is faint and negative and their lives, so far as observation goes, seem little affected by their beliefs. Human personality, however, is a delicate and mysterious thing and its life history cannot be summed up in a rough-and-ready judgment. There is probably more co-operation with the work of the Holy Spirit in most lives than appears on the surface; its results only become apparent very slowly over long periods of time. Here again, and in a more hopeful sense, what is true of the individual is true of the community: its malformation is obvious, its growth is unobtrusive. The unnoticed and hidden character of all growth in grace must be taken into account in any serious judgment of Christianity. Even those many Christians who drift from the Church or reject it are responsive to the grace of their Baptism in some part of their lives and in ways of which they are unaware. Yet when all this is granted, it is still true that full spiritual growth depends on the 'dying life' of the Gospel and is hindered by doubt of its reality and meaning. To what is it that we die?

At the threshold of human life in its wonder and beauty, the Baptismal service lays a stern emphasis on renunciation. The emphasis is startling and bewildering if it is regarded as purely negative. It is in reality a reminder that human nature has a scope even greater than all the great glories of sense and intellect: the true negation and mutilation of its faculties comes from the endeavour to shut itself inside them like a snail in his house of shell. All religion presupposes an existence other than our own to which it reaches out, and in this it is one form of the imaginative expansion which is part of human capacity. But the expansion of religion is accompanied by awe, worship and aspiration: it is a reaching upward to what is higher and better, as well as other, than ourselves, and in this lies the especial character of its demands. Communion with what is above us is like climbing into mountain air, or flying to still higher altitudes: sooner or later, if we trust to natural equipment only, our breath and our heart will fail us and we shall be unable to live in the rare atmosphere. All of us have to some extent experienced this, in contact with someone whom we know to be morally greater than ourselves. We are aware that this contact is a great privilege and good, yet the effort to sustain it is difficult. It braces us and pulls us up, somewhat against our will, into a higher region: we are conscious of the pull and struggle and the new level is unfamiliar. Only our love and admiration can make the effort worth while. But the difficulty would be intensified and the reluctance greater, if we had for a long time rejected the influence of this other and forsaken his company. We might still love him after a fashion. But we should understand and respond to him less easily and should have to part with still more of our habitual selves to achieve any true relationship.

This parable of the human race in its relationship with God perhaps throws some true light on Christian mortification. Our natural impulses are not to be crushed out of us: Christianity is not Stoicism and the Stoic ἀπαθεία is its very antithesis. We die, not to our natural feelings of love, desire, enjoyment, but to the tendency which keeps us wholly to their level and makes them the bourne of our satisfaction. There is something in us which reaches out beyond them and we claim our inheritance in this by the Baptismal renunciation. From this moment the Holy Spirit can begin His work in the soul, remaking it in the Divine likeness and recalling us to our true environment. Yet this sanctification of our whole nature and state cannot be easy or natural. Its end is to make us one with what is higher than ourselves, and although in a sense we do truly love what is higher, the whole self-centred habit of our nature tugs against it. This tendency is a habit, not a function, but the centuries of existence during which the human race as a whole has been going on its own way apart from God, have given the habit a terrifying power. It is a hard and fierce struggle to counteract it and, instead, to respond to the outward and heavenward movement of Divine grace. The first stage in this co-operation appears to be negative; it is a determined rejection of this world's goods and promises as final ends, and the renouncement has to be repeated in one way or another, at every stage of life. Nevertheless there is from the first a positive quality in mortification of which we very slowly become aware. It is the gradual emergence into a new kind of life in which the Being and Presence of God envelop us with an indescribable reality and everything else has a renewed value and beauty because its life is seen to be in Him. This is not any special 'mystical' experience: it appears to be the normal result, in greater or less degrees of clearness, of a steadfast perseverance in self-denial for the love of God, quite apart from any special spiritual gift or capacity.

But the life of grace is not wholly a life of dying, even though the dying has a positive aim and result. It is also, from the beginning, a life of offering and sacrifice, and in this too it is conformed both to the pattern of Christ and to the whole rhythm of the religious consciousness everywhere. In the death-life of mortification the soul renounces all enjoyment of itself and creatures that is apart from God, and the acquirement of this habit means some practical renunciation in ways which vary at different times. In sacrifice, it does more than make this acknowledgement of God's supremacy: it gives back itself and all creatures to Him, as far as lies in its power, by a willed and loving offering. This offering does not always or necessarily mean forgoing. To accept joy without scruple, uniting it with the infinite joy of the Divine Heart, is as natural to the consecrated life as the acceptance of sorrow. But Christian sacrifice, whether of joy or sorrow, has always this characteristic, that it can never be made in isolation. It is always an offering united with the perfect and entire self-offering of Jesus Christ: through Him, again, each individual sacrifice is one with that of believers everywhere, and with all who in good faith, whatever their religion, are offering their lives to God. Thus the Christian life which begins for each individual with Baptism finds its maturity in sacrifice, and its centre in the Holy Communion. The Lord's Supper is the central service of the Christian Church, not only because Christ is the Food of the needy soul but because we are here admitted to the greatest of all privileges, to be sharers in the Divine self-giving. Each Christian, in his measure, here offers himself for humanity, giving himself for the worship of God and the service of his fellows.

Wide indeed and free is the world into which even the least attempt to keep the Baptismal promises leads the

Christian soul. But entry to this world can only be won, and life continued in it, by the steady practice of intercourse with God. The life of grace is characterized for us in many parts of the New Testament, but all its observed qualities spring from one invisible root and are nourished imperceptibly, by prayer. Our Lord gave few specific commands about their use of time to His disciples and almost all these are concerned with their prayer-life. They are 'always to pray': their prayer is to be confident, detailed, and persevering: it will determine their attitude to the world around them and will unite them with Himself and with the Father in a deep and inseparable relationship. He gave them a pattern of prayer which could be indefinitely applied and adapted to all times and circumstances. The ideal Christian life, in all its depth, breadth, and inclusiveness, in all its boundless adaptability, can be studied, better perhaps than anywhere else, in the Lord's Prayer. Its marks are conscious, loving dependence upon God and faith in His Eternal Being; steadfast adherence to His Will and purpose: simple and confiding prayer to Him for all our needs: love of our fellows without any self-satisfaction or sense of superiority, but with an admission of our state of indebtedness. Its attitude is one of humble and simple realism, knowing the sad truths of evil and of human weakness, yet looking outward and upward to a Heaven where God reigns, and assured that He is a loving Father.

It will be worth while to spend a little time in reflection on this prayer. Its outlook is strikingly different from any form of materialist philosophy. Yet it may leave us, in the end, with a philosophy of life better able to withstand the most penetrating examination, and with our reason, as well as our desires, more deeply and truly satisfied.

Chapter Nine

THE LORD'S PRAYER

The Lord's Prayer brings us face to face with the greatest question of all religion: How should we think of God? Is He to be thought of as that which is unknown; so far removed and different from humanity that all our ideas of Him are misleading and best reduced to a minimum? or are our mental pictures, not simply a projection of our own likeness, but an adumbration of truth? The question has been answered in different ways, and it is true that as we advance in prayer our best thought of God is a silence. But for the beginning of our prayer-life, when we are learning our way into the Presence of God, we must affirm something of His Nature, and our Lord's teaching is large in its affirmations. He takes the very simplest and most universal of anthropomorphic ideas about God and makes it the foundation of prayer. We need not fear the image or regard it as something which had a use for humanity at certain stages, but is unprofitable and even dangerous now. It is not like the brand Excalibur on one side of which was written 'Take me' and on the other 'Cast me away'. It expresses in human and limited terms as much as is humanly possible of an eternal relationship: our highest conception and experience of human father-hood is a faint, but a real likeness of all that 'Fatherhood' means in God.

Our Lord might have chosen a different course in His

teaching and might have laid no emphasis on the thought of God as Father. There were tendencies in the Hebraism of His time which led away from it. He could have chosen to dwell wholly on the ineffable majesty of the Divine Name, or on the Divine Wisdom, and could have surrounded the Divine Nature with unapproachable awe. Instead of this, He has commanded us, before everything else, to have a simple and personal attitude towards God as our Father. This is to be the beginning of all our knowledge of Him and is even to precede any clear affirmations of His Reality and Eternity. The child knows his mother obscurely, by touch and tenderness, long before he has any clear awareness of what she is like: so man, if he is to be nourished in the highest part of his nature, must reach out lovingly to the Highest, and must practise an intercourse which he will find to be real.

Prayer thus begins where, in a fuller sense, it ends, in a tender and affectionate relationship which is the source of strength and power. This relationship in its true character is made possible by our union with Jesus Christ, in which we share His perfect Sonship. But if the desire and (in some measure) the capacity for intercourse with God are a part of human nature, then all prayer has an element of true knowledge from the beginning. This dim faith-knowledge is wholly congruous with reason, but it is not a branch of reason or even its reward and climax: it might rather be thought of as the extension of our *a priori* knowledge into the realms of the supernatural. It is knowledge, feeling and love; but it remains dim and indescribable because it is directed towards an object inconceivably great. This obscure knowledge provides the ground in which the Holy Spirit works and where our experience of God grows silently. It would be hardly right to call it a capacity for prayer, but it is a potentiality; it is this which the Holy

Spirit uses when He prays in us and frames our lips and hearts to the 'Abba, Father' of our Lord's prayer.

The intellect, nevertheless, has a part in prayer and it is a very important part. The first act of trust in the Divine Fatherhood is followed immediately by the great affirmation 'Who Art in Heaven', which might be called the metaphysical basis of Christianity. It founds and establishes our mental and moral life upon great mysteries— upon the Reality and Transcendence of God and His Existence apart from ourselves. We are on Earth, He is in Heaven. The belief in a realm of existence, far above our own, where God dwells, is placed at the beginning of the Lord's Prayer that it may underlie and determine ours. Its localization is an image natural and necessary to us and it would be rash to say that such a mental picture has no connection at all with reality. Value it certainly has. It expresses for us, not only the transcendence of God but His power to realize completely our longings after a limitless and enduring beatitude. He is the Good, the object of intellectual search: what the visible heaven is to our senses, God is to our mind and soul.

The following clauses of the Lord's Prayer carry our thoughts of this supreme reality further. They declare that in Heaven God is worshipped, reigns and is served by spirits whose will is in union with His. Man is the crown of the visible creation; but when he comes to God in prayer, his aim must be simply to reproduce on earth an attitude of heart, mind and will which exists already in another sphere. Man is not presented to us as the centre of the universe or Earth as of unique importance in the eyes of God. The prodigal son is not the only son, the lost sheep is one of many: the angels in heaven rejoice over the penitent. It is a humbling and tranquillizing thought that we must enter into a relationship of harmony with God which other created beings know and have never broken. We are part of a great order in which certain characteristics are common to all: adoration and obedience and activity of service. It is a cosmic order in which the Kingdom and Will of God are being continually fulfilled according to His Nature, and where love is the unifying bond, expressing and renewing itself continually.

There has been a breach in this order, a rebellion and self-assertion in which man has become deeply involved. The traditional belief that he was not its primary author is in keeping with probability; but he has been profoundly affected by it and the gracious mystery of the Incarnation has made him the centre and starting-point of its healing. The second half of the Lord's Prayer is chiefly concerned with the results of this breach and with the needs of those called to co-operate in mending it. In the first half of the Prayer we associate ourselves with the Will of God and give ourselves to His service: in the second we admit our incapacity to serve Him without His gift, aid, and pardon, at every point of our lives.

Imagine a man to be engaged in a very serious and responsible work—some great piece of engineering, perhaps, on which the well-being and security of many others will depend. His needs would be many and varied, if the work is to be well done. Chief among them would be a regular and dependable supply of food for himself and his co-workers: a very clear realization of his own faults and limitations in relation to his special task, yet a conviction that in spite of these he will have the power to go forward and complete the work; a clear appreciation, too, of the faults and weaknesses of those who are sharing his task, his human instruments; yet a power of seeing beyond their faults and working harmoniously with these imperfect colleagues and subordinates. Lastly, he will need preservation from dire external misfortune, caused by malice or accident, which may suddenly threaten to overwhelm and annihilate in a moment the great work which he is accomplishing.

The comparison has its value. Every good man is engaged in such a work as this, and has a share in the building of God's Kingdom upon earth; every Christian is committed to it by a solemn contract which brings a special responsibility. Within a wide field of differing vocation, Christian men and women are united in the same task, and they have the same needs as the worker just described. The petitionary clauses of the Lord's Prayer tell us to ask confidently for the fulfilment of these needs.

We ask food for our bodies, provided without an atmosphere of anxiety. 'Give us each day our bread for the coming day.' In making this petition for ourselves we make it for others and commit ourselves to an 'economic' attitude of service and responsibility. To 'feed the hungry', in however indirect a way, is a primary Christian duty. But to do our work as Christians we need more than bodily sustenance: we need Divine sustenance as well. The principle which underlies any rule of fasting and abstinence is right, however much its practice needs to be moderated. It is a corrective to natural self-indulgence, but it is much more than that; it asserts the inadequacy to our needs of all earthly bread. Our food is necessary to us and yet inadequate, as our Lord says plainly. 'I have meat to eat that ye know not of.'[1] 'My meat is to do the Will of Him that sent me.'[2] The soul needs the closest contact with God if it is to do anything for God. In asking for our daily bread, we ask for the spiritual sustenance, through prayer, reading, and sacrament, which each of us needs for his special task. Without it, our life will be starved at its roots,

[1] St. John, iv, 32.   [2] id., iv, 34.

and it is vital to recall this our deepest need with special seriousness from time to time in each year. A life too entirely full of work and activity is in danger of lacking its true spiritual bread. Our Lord took especial pains, it would seem, to draw His followers' minds upwards, from the necessity of bodily sustenance to the thoughts of its inadequacy. It was almost immediately after the Feeding of the Five Thousand that He startled and shocked them by the description of Himself as the Bread of Life, the food of the soul in time and eternity.

Christ is the Food of our souls; but we must not limit His operation. He is the Lord not only of our bodily and spiritual life but of those intellectual and aesthetic capacities which are part of God's gift to us. These, too, need food, if the whole man is to be available for His service, and we must be careful that in our very desire to serve Him faithfully we do not impoverish our reasoning powers and our sense of beauty. There is here an especial danger for religious persons and a cause of great harm and discredit to Christianity. Ordinarily speaking, the mind and the aesthetic sense are to be developed and used. If this is so, it will be part of our prayer to ask for such nourishment of these faculties as is best for each of us: we shall expect the silent direction of the Holy Spirit in what we read, choose, and love. This does not mean limitation or scrupulosity in our likings. The Divine Wisdom is gladdened by all that is good and He finds good in a great variety of places. All we need do is to bring our intellect, our sense of beauty, our creative impulse, within the sphere of His holy influence and ask that here too He will give us our daily bread.

The second of the petitionary clauses brings us even closer to the supernatural values and standards which are to transform our whole life. 'Forgive us our debts. . . .

Forgive us our trespasses—as we forgive.' This is a different region from that of the ordinary experience which life brings. In matters of money and property we do not expect, or even desire, the remission of our debts: it is part of our self-respect to pay them, even when the creditor is our friend. In the sphere of law and justice, although the final aim may be remedial, we regard due punishment for offences as equitable and right. But in the life of grace all is different, and we see this clearly in the realm of forgiveness. The grace of Christ does not only complement and transcend our standards: it rewrites them in its own terms and, in doing so, conforms them to a deeper truth. Our Lord's meaning is not confined to the forgiveness of actual injuries. Vitally important as this is, it comes from a frame of mind which is positive and habitual: it comes from the realization of our own complete indebtedness. We are debtors to God in the extremest sense: we can never pay back to Him what He gives and our only possible attempt at repayment is an ungrudging generosity towards our fellow-men.

The wonderful discourse in the sixth chapter of St. Luke is a fuller development of this theme. In the short form of the Beatitudes which is found here, our Lord gives a sketch of the life which makes no claims. He then pronounces a condemnation of terrifying solemnity upon its opposite. 'Woe unto you that are rich for you have your consolation . Woe unto you that are full, for you shall hunger.' Continuing with the significant words 'But I say unto you *that hear*' he draws an amazing picture of the forgiving and giving life, unreserved in its generosity, ever giving more than is asked and more than necessity requires. Here we see the grace-filled life operating at its fullest energies and highest power, and it is a life, our Lord tells us, which resembles the life of God.

It follows that this self-giving must be varied and many-sided, after the example of the Divine self-giving as we see it poured forth in creation. Gifts of money, time, thought, companionship, the ungrudging lending of our minds for the use and help of others, will all be demanded of us continually, and from time to time the gift too of our readiness to suffer. In this way the life of every Christian who has made a true donation of himself will be conformed, not only to the creative self-giving of God the Holy Spirit, but to the Cross of Christ in its sacrificial fruitfulness. It will probably contain short or long periods of apparent uselessness and neglect, when all our efforts at self-donation seem to go unrewarded. This is to be expected and, as far as we can, welcomed, because it traces a little more deeply the Divine lineaments in our lives. Yet such a life is never wholly and permanently 'rejected of men'. Generosity, sooner or later, calls out love and generosity in response. In proportion as it seeks no return, the generous life is in the long run superabundantly rewarded, often by unsolicited human love and gratitude, and always by the Spirit and power of God Himself, inflowing into generous souls.

The note of sober humility in the clauses that follow is not surprising. Christian life in society is a life of richness and beauty, unbounded in its possibilities, and yet also immensely difficult. The grace of God can only find free play in human personality when personal claims are subordinated; and, paradoxical though it seems, this subordination is the only way to a strong and stable personal life. Here, where the main battle-ground of every life lies, there are no swift or easy victories. An attempt to cut short the conflict by unqualified submission to other people may be more disastrous than any self-assertion. There is a legitimate guarding of personality, as a trust held for God, and apparent unselfishness can be an evasion of responsibility. Yet the distinction between true and false unselfishness is often very difficult to make. Submissiveness to others, a yielding temper which reaches the point of folly, may sometimes be required of us, and at other times a stubborn resolution which has the appearance of self-will. The only real solution lies in the habit of prayer. It may bring no immediate answer to the question, but it guards personality at its true centre of union with God, and the very desire to know His will is a simplification.

But though the choice of action may often be difficult the real choice is always the same. It is a choice between self-seeking in one or other of its myriad forms, and self-abnegation. The temptation to choose the former is almost overwhelming, and more depends on a successful resistance than can possibly be realized at the time: it is, in the deepest sense, a matter of life and death. The exclusion, little by little, of selfish aims, frees human character to fulfil its highest possibilities and to grow up unhindered into the light. Without this free room and expansion towards the highest, it is a thwarted and stunted growth. Where the issues are all-important, it is common prudence to realize our weakness and to avoid, when we can lawfully do so, the occasions of danger. 'Lead us not into temptation' is the prayer not of cowardice, but of self-knowledge, and without a measure of self-knowledge the best gifts will prove useless.

This war between lower and higher, between limitation and expansion, is a part of any life which is set towards good, and its especial intensity in the Christian life is only to be expected. The very life of God is dwelling in the soul, drawing and enabling us to participate in it: the battle between this Divine life and our natural self-centredness is fierce and prolonged. The description of the con-

flict as the war 'between grace and nature' can hardly be
bettered, and for a full and penetrating description of the
two kinds of life, with their contrasting characters and
aims, we still turn to the great Third Book of the 'Imita-
tion of Christ'. 'Nature' in these chapters is the self-
portrait of Everyman. Many of the characteristics—
curiosity, the love of beautiful things, the love of company
and conversation—are not bad in themselves. They may
even reappear, at a later stage in the spiritual life, transformed and given a new quality and a new direction. But
so long as these natural human qualities are used primarily for the gratification of self, they make true growth
impossible. The choice of 'Nature' which 'hath always self
for her end' results finally in self-destruction.

Conflict, which is the law of the good life everywhere, is
thus deepened and intensified in Christianity. Here as elsewhere, the laws of the spiritual world conform to the
general pattern of human experience even where they
transcend it. The war between grace and nature in the
individual corresponds, at a higher level, to the warring
tendencies which divide human society. Social life has a
double movement, centrifugal and centripetal, a tendency
for component parts to fly away into isolation, and a contrasting movement which draws them to a centre and into
close association with each other. The endurance and
fruitfulness of any society depend on this second and positive movement: the attempt to extend it over ever wider
areas, with varying success and frequent failure, makes a
large part of human history. For the society, as for the
individual, there is no uniform solution. The associations
which are achieved either by personal tyranny or by stan-
dardization of life are in the end most disastrous of all.
True social life only exists where each part of a strongly
knit community has a tough and fertile life of its own, with

free play and room for its especial characteristics. Variety to the point of eccentricity, unity to the point of inflexibility, are the marks of a good society, and in this our human associations resemble the wide and varied life of plant and animal which surrounds them.

This free and varied unity is not only one of the great means of human happiness: it is the way of human survival. Yet it is continually being shattered and torn asunder by the violently disruptive force of self-seeking and self-assertion, a force which seems equally triumphant and irresistible on the large and the small scale. No human means can counteract it, not even the highest and best—neither strength and security, nor the most refined culture, nor the observance of religion: for the cure of disease cannot be found wholly within itself. Cure must come from without, by the infusion of some remedial power; only the Spirit of God, moving in the body of society, can arrest its disintegration. This work of the Holy Spirit is not visible, nor even always directly religious in its results. Our Lord Himself laid great emphasis upon its hiddenness but also upon its all-importance and its universal effect. The leaven is hidden in the loaf, but it works there, secretly and silently, 'until the whole is leavened'. Thus when a Christian prays to be kept from temptation he is not praying any timid and exclusive prayer, directed to his personal salvation only. He is praying that the life of grace may be kept quick and unhindered in his spirit, not for his own use but for its Divine work in the whole body of the world.

But if human self-will were the sole enemy it might long ago have capitulated to the sweet approaches of grace; for the good in human nature is very strong. The last petition of the Lord's Prayer presupposes another kind of evil, existing outside ourselves and possessing an evil purpose against which the sole remedy is a cry for rescue. There seems no reason why the power of choice should be limited to human beings, and we cannot deny that the self-centred life—our own direst temptation—may have been chosen in terrible completeness by existences other than ours. Moreover, the full choice of evil seems to include the desire of reproducing itself in others. We can see this happening, to some extent, even in our own experience. Shakespeare carried it perhaps to the limit of human possibility in the character of Iago, and we can dimly imagine it carried further still. It is better that our imagination should ordinarily dwell on good rather than on evil, which has no substantial existence of its own and is a misuse or perversion of good. Yet our Lord's plain teaching is not to be ignored. There are powers in the universe who have made evil their good and wish man to do the same. Even a moment's thought of this throws a terrifying light on our small region of choices: it brings home the fact that prayer is man's most desperate necessity as well as his highest good.

Prayer is the fulfilment of personality and no individual life can grow to completion without it, but it is not a personal or private thing, existing for each of us in isolation. The opening 'Our Father' of the Lord's Prayer gives the note to our prayer-life. Christian prayer is the prayer of the whole body of the Church of Christ, in union with its Head: all our individual and corporate prayers are a childlike repetition of the Lord's Prayer after Him and are taken up by Him into union with His own eternal life of prayer. The realization of this does, in fact, make prayer easier. It shows the reality and value of the 'common' prayer, the daily and weekly services of the Church, and it deepens our understanding of the relation between prayer and sacrifice. The supreme means by which our prayer is taken up into the Lord's and offered with it, is the Holy Eucharist: all the other services of the Church are centred round this, in both their historical origin and their living character. The whole prayer of the Church, not only the service of the Lord's Supper itself, is a memorial of the Passion, and a means of union with the Risen Lord; in every part of it we touch the whole life of Jesus. Liturgical worship is thus immeasurably more than a formal expression, however beautiful, of the interior life. It is in itself an essential and fundamental part of prayer. Our private prayers can only have the depth and the background which they need when they are, as it were, immersed in the prayer of the Church and in the Eucharistic sacrifice. This can be largely an unconscious process, but it is not the less real for that. The Holy Spirit commands certain conditions if His work of remaking us in Christ's likeness is to be possible. Private prayer and self-denial, combined over long periods of time with a share in Christian worship, seem to afford these conditions, in which the whole character can be spiritualized and reborn. There is a twofold encouragement here for our religious life, where we need great encouragement. It is a consoling and enlivening thought that our church-going, however dull and mechanical it sometimes feels, is a vital part of prayer: on the other hand, the knowledge that our private prayers are set deep in the life of a vast community is a great help to perseverance. We 'pray with the most: for where most pray is Heaven', even in our most withdrawn and solitary prayer. The more fully our will and attention are set upon God, the more completely thereby we are one with an innumerable company, lost like ourselves in adoration and love.

Chapter Ten

CONCLUSION

Even the simplest thought on the Lord's Prayer is like dropping a plummet into immeasurable depths. The content of Christianity is inexhaustible and there is no direction in which St. Paul's phrase 'the unsearchable riches of Christ' cannot be applied. The influence of grace is not restricted to any part of human nature, not even to the moral or religious part. Being itself life, and life at its fullest and richest, it permeates every corner and cranny of the lesser life which it redeems, and in the act of doing so, reorganizes it into a richer unity than the original bare identity of self-consciousness, or than the oneness of a common humanity. In the true Christian character, whether of an individual or of a community, there are no isolated compartments, yet no arbitrary subordination of one part to another. Everything is universalized, not by a rigid systematization, but by the one life that flows through all: every part has laws and powers of its own by which it grows in a real independence. We easily understand this in simple and practical things, where concentration on the matter in hand is an absolute necessity, and conscious preoccupation, even with the highest thoughts, is fatal to the work's excellence. The same direct and full concentration is essential in the realms of thought and knowledge. Philosophy, art, and science are each in this sense 'autonomies', and their free growth, undirected by a conscious ulterior purpose, is not only possible but necessary. There is no need for anxiety about the results of this freedom of development, in any sphere. What the whole man is, determines the final quality of his work, and when the whole man is surrendered to 'the penetration of grace', this is truer still, by an exact *a fortiori*. But whether in cooking a dinner, writing a poem, or building a complex structure of thought, the execution requires a free and detached attention to the demands of the special task. The varied activities of humanity must be rich and full in their own development, if they are to be worthy material for the action of Divine grace.

It was perhaps the especial work of Baron Friedrich von Hügel to develop this conception of a true Christian humanism in terms which made it real and living for his own day. Those who learned from him in the first place a new vision of Christianity as something infinitely rich and inclusive can never be sufficiently grateful. But his teaching was not new: it was a rediscovery and re-emphasis of what is implicit in the Gospels, where the very image of the leaven presupposes the value of the loaf. One of the commonest temptations of religious people, as von Hügel pointed out in a great and well-known letter,[1] is to live within a little circle of religious observance and to neglect the general cultivation of their powers. In the end, they cramp and diminish the spiritual life itself which they are striving to cultivate; for this needs everything which the individual has, if it is to find its full expansion. The free and paradoxical spirit of Christianity, always at play between truth and counter-truth, demands at once a deep inner detachment from the things of this world and a strenuous perfection in the use of them.

But it is not enough to say that there are no isolated compartments in the full Christian life. Christianity itself,

[1] Letter to G.G., September 1919.

as we have already seen, is not an isolated compartment. The work of God in Christ is universal in two ways. It is the salvation of all mankind from destruction by a redeeming act, prepared for and wrought out in history: and it is the penetration of all human life, individual and social, by the life of the Risen Jesus. In both these ways it is the full and perfect utterance, in our earthly conditions, of God Who is Love, and cannot be detached and isolated from other expressions of that love. The Christian religion is a part, although the crowning part, of a great world of spiritual knowledge and experience, out of which, humanly speaking, it has grown, and to which it has constantly been indebted. Christians have no monopoly of prayer and vision of God: they have the great and solemn privilege of knowing, with conscious awareness, the Incarnate Lord and of being united with Him in the intimacy of conscious service. It is clear that our Lord chose for His special instrument the 'little company of faithful people' which was the nucleus of the Christian Church, and that His choice was of a lasting character, extending far into the future. St. Augustine's words, however, remain true even apart from their particular context: 'Many who seem to be outside the Church are within it';[1] and those righteous souls whom circumstance has placed outside the Christian body have their share in the redeeming work of Christ. The special vocation of the Church does not detach it, but rather, unites it with the whole spiritual history of mankind.

It is, partly, the clear realization of this truth which gives much of early Christian literature such great nobility and dignity. The writers recognized a religious sense in man, inseparable from a complete humanity. In spite of the sins and horrors of idolatry they were convinced that no part of the human race had ever been entirely cut off

---

[1] Multi qui foris videntur, intus sunt, *De Baptismo*, v. 38.

CONCLUSION

from God and from the light of His revelation; they were
ready to appeal, as St. Paul frequently does,[1] to this past
religious experience as a valid ground of faith and hope.
In full consciousness of what they were doing, they allowed
and accepted the influence of pagan literature at its highest,
claiming it by right and title as part of the riches of Christ.[2]
The same thought inspired the finest Christian humanism
of the Renaissance. It is difficult to hold an even balance
between the uniqueness of Christianity and its close fellowship with all goodness; but it is essential that the balance
should be held and full justice done to both truths.
'Spirituality is a common possession of all mankind,'[3] and
Christian thought has been richest and most fruitful whenever it has realized this most fully.

It follows that the characteristic temper of Christianity
is positive and appreciative rather than critical. It is prone
to include rather than to reject, gathering all that is good
into a rich and fertile synthesis. The Church can say like
Antigone:

My nature is to love with them that love,
Not hate with them that hate.

Yet the Christian can never merely adapt himself to his
surroundings and will sometimes be in irreconcilable conflict with them. It is not his especial task, as a Christian,
to combat systems of politics or philosophy, as if his religion were a rival system, though he will have a natural
predilection for such systems as leave men free to think,
choose, and act. But he must testify, even to martyrdom,
not only for the truth of the Christian revelation, but for

[1] Acts xiv, 14–17, xvii, 23–28. Romans i, 17–25.
[2] e.g. Minacius Felix, *Octavius*, C. 20, 1. Clement of Alexandria,
Exhortation to the Greeks, C. 6. St. Gregory Nazianzen, *Funeral Oration
on St. Basil*, C. 11.
[3] '*The Personality of Christ*', Dom Anscar Vonier, O.S.B.

the truth and validity of the religious consciousness everywhere, and for the moral revelation which has accompanied its growth. This has perhaps never been more strongly exemplified than in our own days. Communism, where it bases itself upon Karl Marx, makes a fatalistic materialism the basis of society: the atheist school of Existentialism, though it lays a valuable insistence on the creative nature of choice, denies God as completely as the Marxist, and thus cuts away quite arbitrarily half of human experience. Christian opposition to both of these is absolute and inevitable: yet it must at the same time be humbly penitent and discerning. No theory or way of life, however false and harmful, ever gained widespread acceptance without containing some germ of a neglected truth. The task of Christian thinkers is to draw out these truths from the confusion and negation which surround them, and to connect them once more with a belief in the Divine government of the world. Modern atheism, like Shelley's, often springs from wrong thoughts of God for which Christian teachers themselves may have been partly responsible. Today these wrong conceptions go very deep, and learning as well as prayer are needed to undermine them. The recovery of faith in God is the first essential, if the Christian religion is to be brought home to a generation in great need.

There is a passage in Bishop Stubbs's Inaugural Lecture as Professor of Modern History at Oxford which, although spoken more than eighty years ago, is still very significant .It emphasizes the value and importance of the whole natural order, whether studied in the Natural Sciences or in human affairs, and at the same time, the directing yet wholly unconstraining character of the Divine Providence. Coming from one of the deepest students of history who have ever taught, the words have especial weight, and they reach us charged with a new solemnity by the events which have followed them. 'There is, I speak humbly, in common with Natural Science, in the study of living History, a gradual approximation to a consciousness that we are growing into a perception of the workings of the Almighty Ruler of the world: that we are growing able to justify the Eternal Wisdom and to approve ourselves His children; that we are coming to see, not only in His ruling of the Church in her spiritual character, but in His over-ruling of the world—to which His act of redemption has given a new and all-interesting character to His own people—a hand of justice and mercy, a hand of progress and order, ever leading on the world to the better, but never forcing, and out of the evil of man's devising, ever bringing that which is good.'

There is not only a deep piety in this passage, precious as that is: there is a stable and wise philosophy of life based upon strong intellectual foundations. It would seem at first sight that this secure faith might be taught best through a pure Theism, and that the Christian doctrine of God, in its fullness, should at any rate be postponed. Yet experience bears out what the instinct of Christendom feels to be right. Our Lord is the Door and He is the Way: it is through the conviction of the Divinity as well as Humanity that faith in a living God becomes solid and firm. The teaching of Christianity means the steady, patient, resourceful teaching of Christian doctrine, as a revelation of the Being and Action of God, and in relation to the whole of His self-disclosure in Nature and History. It is a task which demands continual study, for Christianity has a rich intellectual as well as spiritual inheritance. It requires also unwearied sympathy and flexibility in presentation. The false conception of dogma as something which limits and hardens true religion can often be

CONCLUSION

only very gradually broken down, and no one can at any moment be forced beyond his present stage. The teaching of Christian doctrine is governed by the same laws as all other teaching. The teacher's task is threefold: to make his own knowledge as deep and sound as possible, to be himself habitually a learner, and to vary and adapt his teaching to the needs of individuals. When he has done this he can do no more—the results are not in his power; and this is nowhere truer than in the highest regions of thought. All which the teacher and pupil can achieve by their co-operation is to prepare the soil and make response to the work of the Holy Spirit easier; the full growth and productivity of the mind depends wholly on this response. It is the Wisdom that 'cometh from above' Who vivifies and fructifies thought as it grows, and leads it up into the air and light of a true conclusion.

Ascension Day,
1949

INDEX